# THE CHURCH QUIZ

## WHAT GRADE DOES GOD GIVE YOUR CHURCH FOR GROWING HIS KINGDOM?

## Jud Boies

A **GOALS SERIES** BOOK

BUSINESS **GOALS** PUBLISHING

Business Goals Publishing
P.O. Box 2661
Granite Bay, CA  95746
Businessgoals.org

Copyediting and production: Jennifer Edwards (jedwardsediting.net)
Book and cover design: Dave Eaton
Author photo: Bayside Church, Granite Bay, CA


ISBN  979-8-9860575-3-8 (PRINT)
ISBN 979-8-9860575-4-5 (EBOOK)
ISBN 979-8-9860575-5-2 (AUDIO)

Printed in the United States of America

*"I am extremely thankful for **Church Goals**, a unique program that has given us the tangible resources and tools to know what our church should be doing to reach more people. The principles and ideas behind it are so simple and practical. You don't need a big budget or a ton of volunteers to implement each step. The modules allow you to start where you are, showing you how to effectively do church on Sunday, start a new ministry, or improve an existing one. It's not just theory but practical steps for me as a pastor to take each week as we build our church. I highly recommend **Church Goals** to any pastor who wants to reach more people for Jesus."*

**—Gary Greeno, Senior Pastor**
**Horizon Christian Fellowship, Stockton, CA**

*"Jesus says, 'Ask and it will be given to you; seek and you will find;' (Matthew 7:7). The Lord has truly been faithful through **Church Goals** and Jud Boies. As a diocese that had been in decline with aging congregations, **Church Goals** has provided just the right level to encourage our clergy and lay leaders, challenge my leadership, and help us all get to the next level. I highly recommend this ministry and pray for the Lord's blessing on you!"*

**—The Rt. Rev. Dr. Eric Vawter Menees**
**Bishop of the Anglican Diocese of San Joaquin, Fresno, CA**

*"**Church Goals** brings together top-level strategies with boots-on-the-ground practice. **Church Goals** not only knows what healthy churches need but shows you how to get there."*

**—Kyle Thomsen, Lead Pastor**
**Life Community Church, Roseville, CA**

*Thank you to the hundreds of churches that have been part of the **Church Goals** program and have provided feedback to help the next church grow and become stronger. And thank you to Larry and Chris for asking me the right questions.*

# CONTENTS ✎

# FOREWORD

## by Mark Clark

I was reading a book the other day, and the author pointed out that in the 1990s and 2000s if you went to a Christian conference and did a breakout session on Worship, End Times, or whatever, it was packed, but other topics weren't as interesting to Christian leaders. Today, he said, it's different. Now if you do a breakout on one topic over all others, it is packed, that being *discerning the will of God for the direction of your church and life.* I agree that this is a deep desire in all of us and should be, and I don't know a book that does it better in regard to ministry than *The Church Quiz.* I only wish I'd had this book when I was trying to discern my role and calling in life.

As a nineteen-year-old, I was working at Michaels, an arts and crafts store, and planned to go into the film industry as an actor, writer/director, or whatever they would let me do. I was already signed up and had started college. One day, I went away with three friends, and they all sat me down and said, "We think you are going in the wrong direction in your life. You should go to Bible College instead and become a pastor because you have the gifts of leadership, evangelism, teaching, and apostolic thinking—and God could use those for really cool things. And the weird thing is that we all felt God tell us this completely separate over the last few weeks." I laughed and said I don't even know what you are talking about or how I would do that. A week later, I went away to a friend's house for a weekend, and her father said to me out of nowhere, "God told me you are supposed to go into ministry and become a pastor."

What?

Crazy.

I ignored them and pushed it off, and then one day, I was standing in Michaels putting away Christmas wreaths (in August), and all of a sudden, I felt this pressure on my chest and started to cry. I couldn't control it! It was all about this question of what I was going to do with my life, and I realized God was calling me. At that point in my life, I had no ability to discern what God was asking me to do in my life and needed others to get my attention. Once they did, my life took off. I was finally doing what I was designed to do. But in order to get there, I needed others to guide me. What was all that about?

*Discernment.*

We discern things and make decisions every day for about a hundred different things, but then there is the discernment needed to figure out *who we are* and *how we fit* into this world. And when we discover that, we are filled with meaning and purpose, and direction.

All of this is true about us as individuals, but it is also true about us collectively—as the Church and as *local churches*. And that is where Jud Boies is brilliant. He has developed a way to help us figure out exactly what we should be doing as leaders to make our biggest contribution to the Kingdom of God. But not only that, Jud offers something better: practical questions that produce an actual pragmatic system that you can apply to your church tomorrow. His **Church Goals** program has helped hundreds of pastors and ministry leaders figure out who they are and what they are supposed to be doing in the world and with their church. And when that happens, churches fly!

*The Church Quiz* helps us keep the main thing the main thing—the Gospel and how it connects to lost people. It guides us on how to make disciples by preparing, growing, expanding, and sustaining ministry that is actually effective; how to leverage the gifts and talents in your church to see it grow in a healthy way. I can't thank Jud enough for this book because it lays out exactly how to reach new people and, more importantly, *how to think as a church* in an ongoing way about how to reach the lost. As we look closely into our own church, we can see where we are doing this well and where we are missing the mark. We then make adjustments in everything from what we preach to the language we use and everything in between.

This book is theologically profound and practical in every way. It will one hundred percent help you as a leader to make your church better. No question. If it doesn't, Jud will give you your money back. (He doesn't know I was going to say that, so hopefully, he doesn't edit that out.) This is one of the most practical and clear ministry books I have ever read that brings years of experience to the table and lays out exactly how you can apply all of it to your ministry, in your city, in your way.

What a gift to the Church in every way. Enjoy!

And then pass it on.

**Mark Clark**
Senior Campus Pastor, Bayside Church, Granite Bay, CA
Founding Pastor, Village Church, Canada

# INTRODUCTION

Have you ever questioned everything God has done in your life? Do you wonder if you're misunderstanding what you think God is calling you to accomplish? What are the right questions to ask that will keep you on track and help you overcome the obstacles standing in your way?

A short time ago, I began doubting what I believed God was calling me to accomplish. I was discouraged and scared about my future, questioning everything God had done in my life up to that point. Surely, God had made a mistake, or maybe it was me. Then I met with two close friends who asked me a series of questions. These were Holy Spirit-driven questions that got right to the point. As I heard each question and answered it honestly and confidently, two things happened. First, I felt sheepish and embarrassed that I would question where God had brought me. Second, I realized I hadn't been asking myself the right questions — the questions my two friends had asked, which would have kept me focused and able to tackle obstacles that were threatening to derail me.

Chances are, if you are reading a book called The Church Quiz, you are likely a pastor of a church or a ministry leader who wonders, "Why aren't things going the way I want them to?" Moral of the story? You have to know the right questions to ask, seek the answers, and be willing to make the necessary changes even if the solution is risky or hard.

Like my two friends, I will ask you very pointed questions about your calling, your church, and what God wants you to accomplish in your role. You may think some questions offensive and wonder, "What right do you have to question me?" You might find some questions very difficult because you know the answer itself is difficult to face. That's okay. The important thing is to be introspective and honest in getting to the answer.

I know some of your answers will be, "No, we don't do that," or "Why would we want to do that?" Regardless of your response, please ask the next question: "Should we make any changes in direction based on our answer to the question?" For example, say the question is, "Are we going after the people who live near our church but don't go to church and don't know Christ?" If your answer is "no," ask the follow-up question: "Should we go after them?" Hopefully, YES is the answer that instantly pops in your head, and you get an overwhelming feeling or a passion for going after them. The next question would then be, "What changes should we make to go after them?"

There was another significant outcome from the meeting I had with my friends. Every answer was between God and me; only I provided the answer! My friends didn't give opinions regarding the questions they asked. They simply asked the question and waited for my response. When they did, an answer instantly popped in my head—one consistent with everything I knew to be true about God and what He had already done in my life.

My prayer has been for God to inspire me to ask you the right questions and that you will hear the right answers. So, before you read one more sentence, please stop and ask the Holy Spirit to help you answer each question.

Let's practice right now. As I ask you these questions, does an instant response come to mind? Is that response consistent with how you believe God wants you to answer the question?

☐ Does God want you to accomplish something significant in your lifetime?

☐ Do you think God has equipped you to accomplish something significant?

☐ Might you accomplish this through your church or where He has placed you?

☐ Do you think God will use your past experiences, expertise, and giftings to accomplish whatever it is He wants you to accomplish?

☐ Do you think we are called to reach the lost and make disciples?

☐ Have you been doing all the right things to accomplish what God would like you to accomplish? Might you need to make a few adjustments?

If you've been questioning your calling, wondering what's next for you and your church, are concerned about the future, or are looking for some encouragement, please work through the questions in this book. I believe they will lead you to the right pathway, affirm your calling, and encourage you to press on to accomplish something significant and meaningful for God's Kingdom.

Oh, and at the end of each chapter, you'll find a section called, "You might want to consider…." It provides potential solutions to each question asked. In every case, seek what God is calling you to do in response to the questions. He may be leading you to consider what's listed at the end of the section or something different. Follow His wisdom and guidance.

To read this book in under thirty minutes with some degree of value, simply ask and answer the bolded questions on each page. Alternatively, you can run through all the questions in chapter 15. Answer them and consider the tips for solutions, and you'll be able to affirm your calling, the direction of your church, and what God wants you to accomplish.

# The 5 Key Questions

Are things going how you hoped and wanted? If you've been asking the questions, "Why do I feel so discouraged?" or "Am I successful at what I'm doing?" or "Why isn't my church or ministry growing?" or "Am I accomplishing what God wants me to accomplish?" you're not alone. At one time or another, many of us wonder if we are on the right path, doing what we felt God calling us to do. Somewhere along the way, we notice things aren't going the way we thought they would. A + B is not equaling C, and we feel let down, discouraged, and a bit lost. Fortunately, you can get back on track, refocused, and on your way to accomplishing what God has for your life by working through these five key questions:

## QUESTION #1—Are you called? (AFFIRM)

Have you confirmed you are where God wants you to be? Or did you orchestrate things on your own to get where you are today?

## QUESTION #2—Are you prepared? (PREPARE)

Are you prepared for what you hope and want to have happen? Will God send you the people you need to achieve the goal?

If what you want or hope for takes place, could it result in a bigger problem or disaster because you aren't ready? Could God be holding off giving you what you hope for or want because you aren't prepared?

## QUESTION #3—Do you know how to grow? (GROW)

Are you ready to grow? Do people know you exist? Do you know how to grow numerically, financially, physically, and, most importantly, spiritually to achieve what you hope for?

## QUESTION #4—Are you willing to expand? (EXPAND)

Do you have what people are looking for? Are you willing to expand your world to accommodate getting what you hoped for or wanted? Could you expand how you've been doing things, for example, by changing how you schedule your time? Are you prepared to ask others to help you, for example, by growing the number of key volunteers on your team? If you learn you haven't achieved what you hoped for or wanted because there were some missing components necessary to obtain what you were looking for, are you willing to incorporate some new things into your life? For example, you may learn that you need to add several new ministries to your church for it to grow, or you may need further training to be better equipped to grow and lead your church.

## QUESTION #5—Can you sustain growth? (SUSTAIN)

When you get what you hope for and want, do you know how to sustain it? Do you know that once you reach that goal, there will be new goals? Do you know how to reach those new goals?

Work through these and the related questions in each section. Ask God to show you how you need to add, change, improve, or remove things you're currently doing to get where He wants you to be and achieve what He wants you to accomplish.

# ARE YOU CALLED?

(AFFIRM)

# AFFIRM YOUR CALLING

Most pastors or ministry leaders will tell you that God called them into ministry and the position they currently serve. That "calling" can manifest itself in the form of a vision about your future, several people telling you that you would make a good (fill in the title or role in the church), and opportunities that present themselves to you. Sometimes you just get an idea. The question is, did God gently whisper that idea in your head, or was it your own idea?

We all want to be in God's will and accomplish what He wants us to accomplish. So before you dig deep into what God wants you to achieve, it would be a good idea to confirm (state with assurance) or affirm (state as a fact) that you have been called. Let's make sure you are exactly where God wants you to be.

## KEY QUESTIONS FOR THIS CHAPTER

1. Did God call you into (this) ministry?

2. Is there another place you'd rather be?

3. Do you know what you were called to accomplish?

## #1—DID GOD CALL YOU INTO (THIS) MINISTRY?

The first question to ask when it comes to affirming your mission is whether or not you are called to the place where you are currently. There are two possible answers to this question. Either God called you into ministry because He wants you serving where you are, or you took it upon yourself to take a position that was your own doing, not His. It's critical to determine if you are where God wants you and has called you to serve Him, and I hope these questions help you make that determination. Take a moment and think through the answers for each one.

- ☑ How did you get to the place where you are today?

- ☑ What was the decision process that brought you there?

- ☑ Can you see how each step of the way, whether good or bad, has been used to bring you to the place where you are today?

- ☑ Did you get there because God led you, or did you make things happen on your own?

If you were called, you most likely sensed God's leading to go into ministry or to take a certain position and then watched in awe as He orchestrated everything that allowed you to land where you are today. You may have gone through a series of steps like those listed below to confirm your calling and position. If so, you're probably in the place where you are meant to be, doing the things you are meant to do.

But what if you're unsure whether you were called to this role, ministry, or opportunity to serve the Kingdom? Personally, I use what I call the "Eight Tests" to help me affirm whether or not I should take a position or go for an opportunity and if I'm in the right place according to God's will. You can use these eight tests throughout this book.

# 8 TESTS
## TO AFFIRM YOUR CALLING

1. **Pray about it.** Do I find peace, confirmation, and a general sense of "this just feels right" during prayer?

2. **Seek confirmation while reading Scripture.** While reading Scripture, do I sense God showing me similar situations to what I'm considering?

3. **Seek counsel and direction from people who know a lot about the position.** Who are two or three people in positions of authority I can talk to about the position (i.e., they know a lot about the position—the pros and cons, and they know me)?

4. **Seek counsel and direction from people I trust in the church.** Who are two or three people in positions of authority in the church I can talk to?

5. **Investigate and contemplate the opportunity.** Did the opportunity present itself in a way I felt was from God?

6. **Determine if all the provisions necessary for me to take the position will be met.** Are all provisions for taking the position falling into place, such as the right salary, benefits, vacation time, location, and so forth? Is the timing right in my life for me to take the position so that no relationships will be damaged or severed?

7. **Weigh if it makes sense.** Does it seem like common sense for me to take this position?

8. **Seek the input of my spouse (if married).** Has my spouse run through the tests above, independently from me, and come to the same conclusion?

Going through these tests or similar steps leads to what I would describe as a sense of affirmation. It feels like there is a green light, a "go" message, for each one of them, and I don't sense a check in my spirit about any of them. I take this as an indication that I'm where God has called me to serve Him.

Perhaps you are right where God wants you to be, but you've gone ahead of God and put some things into motion ahead of His will. In that case, do you know where you've gone ahead of God's will and can you unwind it?

I was working with a church that had the vision to build a new building. They agreed that if the financial provision was met from a capital campaign to build the building, they would build it. They went through the capital campaign and did not meet their financial goal but decided to go ahead and build the building anyway with debt financing. They ultimately lost the building.

*The key is to see God's vision for you and allow it*
*to play out according to His will.*

What if you haven't gone through the process of receiving confirmation for where you are now or didn't get a green light on one or more of the tests? It's possible you are where you are because you pushed ahead of your own free will. Perhaps, like Abraham, God gave you a glimpse of your calling and what He wants you to accomplish, but you didn't wait for the right opportunity or timing. You may remember God told Abraham he would be the father of all nations. He even gave him a glimpse of his future. But Abraham and Sarah took it upon themselves to make their ministry happen, outside of God's will, and they created Ishmael. Maybe you have not had the success you've expected because you are not where God wants you to be, or you've pushed ahead on your own.

If this rings true for you, simply ask God for forgiveness for not listening to Him or waiting for His will for your life. Confess you are not where God wants you to be because you pushed ahead on your own accord, ignoring His call and timing. Then ask Him a different set of questions...

- ☑ Where do you want me?
- ☑ How do I get out of the situation I'm in?
- ☑ How can I best serve You at this moment?

If you are where God wants you but you are not experiencing the success you envisioned or expected, it might be that God wants you to make some changes and do some things differently. Is it possible you are in a preparation phase for what God wants to accomplish through you?

# YOU MIGHT WANT TO CONSIDER...

☑ Run through the Eight Tests to confirm, even now, that you are where God wants you to be.

☑ Run all future decisions regarding roles, positions, and opportunities through the same eight tests.

☑ Have the people you are considering hiring or joining your ministry team as volunteers run through the Eight Tests to see if this is where God is calling them to serve.

## #2—IS THERE ANOTHER PLACE YOU'D RATHER BE?

The second thing to affirm is if you are in the right place or not. This question has to do with longings and desires. It's normal to feel some dissatisfaction with a role we're in, but have you ever thought about what you would do if you weren't in the job you're in today? Is there someplace you'd rather be? Do you feel a greater calling to some other place? How do you know if you're in the right place and need to hang in there or if it's time to move on? Is the longing you feel from God to get you to contemplate your position or a temptation from the enemy to lure you away from your mission?

When things aren't going well or how we expected, it's natural to question if we are where God has called us, accomplishing what He wants us to accomplish. Perhaps a better question is, what does God want me to accomplish—not what do I want to accomplish? We can be in the place God has called us, but we're not accomplishing what He wants us to. This really is the key question for many pastors and ministry leaders:

*Are you accomplishing what He wants you to accomplish...in the place where He has placed you?*

God has an interesting way of letting us know we are in the place He wants us. We can go through intense trials and yet have that feeling deep down inside that we are still where we're supposed to be. Sometimes God puts us in places where we must go through trials to accomplish our mission. If we are to grow His Kingdom by reaching the lost in our communities, we will be met with opposition. Other times we create our own trials through our decisions and choices. Sometimes, we're like Peter, being sifted like wheat to see if we can stand strong in our faith. If you are where God wants you, but you aren't accomplishing your mission, keep reading. This book will help you get on the path to success.

If there is someplace you would rather be, you may be in the wrong place. Also, if you've gone through the Eight Tests to confirm your calling and that you are where you're supposed to be and don't get eight out of eight, you are likely in the wrong place.

As long as you don't feel called to be someplace else, keep moving forward, even though things may not be going how you thought they would.

# YOU MIGHT WANT TO CONSIDER...

- ☑ If you get eight out of eight on your calling and the place you are currently serving, that's where God wants you.
- ☑ If someplace else looks tempting, you are probably being tempted.
- ☑ Examine your motives for why you want to be somewhere else.
- ☑ If God is prompting you to move on, determine the best way to move to where you would rather be.

## #3—DO YOU KNOW WHAT YOU WERE CALLED TO ACCOMPLISH?

Okay, you've affirmed that God called you into ministry and placed you as a pastor or ministry leader at your current post. The third question is about knowing what God wants you to accomplish there. Do you know your mission? Does God want you to be there short-term or long-term? Are you working toward a seasonal achievement within your lifetime achievement? Would you agree your mission is probably not to be complacent and see how things play out on their own but requires a variety of action items on your part to make things happen?

Moses was called to a lifetime achievement of freeing God's people from Egypt, leading them into the promised land of Israel, then writing the first five books in the Bible to memorialize those events. Noah was called to a lifetime achievement of restarting mankind. Abraham was called to a lifetime achievement of being the father of all nations. What is your lifetime achievement? Do you know?

Each of the above biblical examples played a series of seasonal achievements into the lifetime achievement. As we read about the seasonal achievements in the Bible, we are reminded that God wants us to have seasonal wins. I like to ask business owners, "Would you rather win one Super Bowl or be part of the team that won the most Super Bowls in history?" Similarly, you may think that your version of winning the Super Bowl would be to get 200 or 500, or 1,000 people to your church. Do you think God wants you to get to whatever that number is and stop? Probably not. Why not look at your future through a different lens? Ask, "What is God calling me to accomplish in this season, in this place where He's placed me," followed by, "that plays into my lifetime achievement?"

In each biblical example, God's servants overcame significant obstacles to achieve their seasonal and lifetime achievements. Do you think it won't be that way for you? You are probably living out a few of the obstacles right now. The Covid-19 pandemic has certainly been an obstacle, but for many churches, it was viewed as an amazing opportunity to reach more people with the Gospel via technology. Racism in the world is certainly an obstacle the Church has to contend with, but we can use it to change hearts and minds. Political and economic issues are also obstacles that so many churches struggle to navigate. Historically, cultural barriers have been trying to prevent God's chosen ones from accomplishing their calling. Perhaps no obstacle is as big as the lack of perceived need for a Savior. The Bible shows us that each time an empire fell, it was preceded by a time when people of the world didn't feel the need for a Savior or God.

Perhaps your calling is more important now than it has ever been. Perhaps God has placed you right where you are to accomplish something significant in your community and for His Kingdom. What would it look like if everyone in your community learned that the Church, and by extension your church, has what they've been missing in their lives?

# YOU MIGHT WANT TO CONSIDER...

(do all three of the following in the order presented)

☐ A personal retreat, spending time in prayer, fasting, and Bible study to hear from God about what you are to accomplish.

- Ask God what your lifetime achievement might be.
- Ask God what your seasonal achievements might be.
- Ask God for specific milestones He wants you to accomplish where He's placed you.

☐ A retreat with key people God has placed around you.

- Ask them to pray that God reveals what He wants your church or ministry to accomplish and for the key leaders in the church, including you, to accomplish.

☐ A Core Group meeting where you ask the Holy Spirit to direct all of the leaders and stakeholders in your church concerning the goals for your church.

- A Core Group meeting is one of the most important meetings you can hold.
- A Core Group meeting asks four key

questions:

> ▸ Why would people like our church?
>
> ▸ Who is God calling us to go after?
>
> ▸ How will we go after them?
>
> ▸ How will each person in the Core
> Group serve?

- If done right, the Core Group meeting will unite your team and your church to the calling God has given you. It also provides the pathway to reach what God has called you and your church to achieve and the people necessary to accomplish that.
- You may want to consider the **Church Goals** program as a resource. The **Church Goals** program provides the details necessary for you to hold a successful Core Group meeting.

Go to churchgoals.org for additional information or scan this QR code:

# 2

# DO YOU KNOW WHO YOUR FLOCK IS?

Who has God entrusted to your care, and what does He expect you to do with them? If you were one of the three servants from Matthew 25:14–30 entrusted with gold, that's pretty valuable. But if He has charged you with something far more valuable, people, what have you done with them? Have you taken the flock of one hundred people and turned it into two hundred? Or are you the one whom He gave fifty people to care for and kept them locked inside your church to protect them but didn't grow your church by one more person?

Matthew 28:19 tells us we are to go out and make disciples of all nations. God clearly wants us to grow our flocks with disciples who obey Christ (v. 20). Matthew 7:19 warns that we will be judged by the fruit we produce. Matthew gives us some key insights into what God calls us to do to produce good fruit. He puts valuable resources (people) into our hands to manage. Like gold, these people have value that can create more value. They can help us attract more people. We are to go out and make disciples. Our success will be based on how much fruit (disciples) we produce.

Matthew also tells us there is a battle for this fruit. Imagine thousands of wild fruit trees that are available for the taking. False prophets are out there trying to spoil the fruit with aphids, disease, and drought (7:15). God wants us to cultivate the orchards and care for and nurture them so the people turn into good fruit—disciples of Jesus Christ who trust and obey Him. God calls us to expand our orchards to incorporate the wild fruit trees to harvest as much good fruit as possible.

In chapter 1, you affirmed (or reaffirmed) your calling. You are confident you're in the right place to serve and understand what God wants you to accomplish (short-term and long-term). It's time to evaluate the people side of things—going out and making disciples. You know what and where, but the really big question is who! Who does God want you to be responsible for, and who will help you with that charge? What trees are you being asked to incorporate into your orchard? What families in your community is God calling you to care for and nurture so the enemy won't get ahold of them?

As a pastor of any sized church, there is tension between shepherding people only in your church and those outside of the walls of your church. Pastors of small churches don't have the staff of large churches, but that doesn't mean large churches do a better job in this area. There is a balance between reaching everyone you can with the gospel of Christ and caring for them once they walk through your doors, including the people already there. Many pastors think it's all they can do to shepherd and care for only those already in their church…but is that all God has called you to do? Let's ask a few questions to find out.

## KEY QUESTIONS FOR THIS CHAPTER

1. Has God charged you to shepherd only those in your church?
2. Whom has God placed in your midst to help you?
3. Is your ministry just about moving peas on the plate?
4. Is your church primarily a hospital for the hurting or a home for the healthy?

## #1—HAS GOD CHARGED YOU TO SHEPHERD ONLY THOSE IN YOUR CHURCH?

What if Christ returns tomorrow and decides He wants to pick a city to call home when He's not traveling around on Earth, and that city is your city? He decides He would like to attend one of the local churches in your town, and He picks your church. As the pastor or someone serving in ministry, His first question might be, "How many people live in your town within five to seven minutes of your church that do not attend on Sunday?" Oh, that's an easy answer for you, I'm sure. You say, "5,000 people, Jesus." He pauses and asks, "Of those, how many do you think I want to hear the gospel message?" Gulp. You know the answer: "All of them."

If all of the people in your entire town heard the gospel and decided to follow Christ, how many of them might attend your church? 10%? 20%? Those seem like very low numbers in Christ's eyes, comparable to those who heard Paul's gospel messages in cities as he traveled. But if your town has 5,000 people who live within five to seven minutes of your church, and you did your best to help them hear the gospel message…then, using those percentages, shouldn't you start planning for a church of 500 to 1,000 people?

The obstacles Paul faced in preaching the gospel 2,000 years ago are no better or worse than today's obstacles. But Paul made it his lifetime achievement to tell as many people as he could about Christ. Did Christ tell Paul only to stop persecuting His people…period? No. He gave him a charge. Acts 9:15 tells us, "But the Lord said to Ananias, 'Go! This man is my chosen instrument to proclaim my name to the Gentiles and their kings and to the people of Israel." And after only a few days, Paul went at once to the synagogues preaching Jesus as the Messiah (v. 20), then to Jerusalem (v. 28), and to everyone who would listen outside the church (13:16).

That should be our charge as well. We should preach and reach everyone we can with Christ's gospel and be prepared to shepherd them when they walk through our doors. Think about your situation. Are you out of bandwidth to think outside your church's four walls? Have you felt overwhelmed and at 100% capacity just taking care of those inside your church? Would you agree it will take significant help from other people to go after the 60% to 90% of people who are not yet in your church? You're not alone if you feel this way. It is overwhelming—hundreds and thousands of lost and hurting people are right across the street. The good news is that if it's God's will to reach the lost and hurting outside your church walls, He will provide the help and support necessary to do so. The **Church Goals** program will help you deploy into service those God is calling to help you.

Are you wondering if God is calling you to reach the lost and hurting in your community? Use the Eight Tests below to resolve this question:

*God, are You calling me to go after as many of the*
*lost families in our community as possible?*

# 8 TESTS
## TO AFFIRM YOUR CALL
## TO REACH THE LOST

1. **Pray about it.** Do I find peace, confirmation, and a general sense of "this just feels right" when I think about reaching the lost in my community?

2. **Seek confirmation while reading Scripture.** Which Scriptures tell me to reach the lost?

3. **Seek counsel and direction from people who know a lot about lost people.** Are people encouraging me to reach the lost in my community?

4. **Seek counsel and direction from people I trust in the church.** Are people in a position of authority in the church encouraging me to reach the lost?

5. **Is there an opportunity?** Are there lost people in my community that need a Savior?

6. **Do I have the provision?** Has God surrounded me with other Christians capable of helping me reach the lost? Maybe a place to bring them (my church or ministry)?

7. **Does it make sense to go after them?** Does it seem like common sense?

8. **Seek the input of my spouse (if married).** Has my spouse run through the tests above, independently from me, and come to the same conclusion about reaching the lost?

# YOU MIGHT WANT TO CONSIDER...

- ☐ Determine how many people in your community are not in church on Sunday and don't know Christ.
  - Start to envision at least 10% to 20% of them coming to your church.
- ☐ Who specifically is God calling you to go after in your community?
  - Couples —helping pre-married or married couples to thrive and prevent divorce?
  - Singles and divorced people?
  - Youth?
  - People looking for community?

## #2—WHO HAS GOD PLACED IN YOUR MIDST TO HELP YOU?

God has put the desire to serve Him in the minds and hearts of many people. Some have been called to be full-time pastors or ministry leaders, but the vast majority are lay people, those who serve God wholeheartedly but still have a day job. They have their own passions, gifts, and callings, and they are right in your midst, eager and ready to help you. You just need to activate and deploy them. But where are they? Do you know who they are? How do you identify them?

There are typically three groups of people God has placed around you to help you with your ministry. They could be new people who either recently met Christ or haven't met Him yet. Some people have been in the church for a while but haven't engaged. Still, others have been leaders in the church, serve in ministry, and are passionate about your ministry or church as a whole. Do a quick assessment of anyone God brings to mind for these groups.

Who has God put in your midst to come alongside you and help grow your ministry? Might the new people invite their friends because they are so excited about this new thing they are involved with called "Christianity"? Might the people who have been in church for a while need further education and development to move into the leadership group where they can contribute to Kingdom expansion? Might God use the leaders in your group to help you grow the ministry? Trust me; you can't do it alone and aren't expected to. What changes do you need to make to identify and recruit these people? How can you get them in the mix?

Sometimes, we play the martyr and fail to take inventory of whom God has put in our midst. We think we're on our own, but they are all around us if we just look for them. I was working with a vice president of a Fortune 500 company who told me he wanted to spend more time in ministry. He was anxious to find out where God might be calling him to spend this extra time working in ministry. I told him it was likely right where God had placed him…at the company where he worked. After the initial shock, it started to make so much sense to him. God had been with him every step of the way as he climbed the corporate ladder at the company. He had amassed a great reputation and had significant influence and affluence. He was excited to see how God would use him right where He placed him. One of the first things I asked him to do was to take an inventory of the people God had placed around him. He was surprised to learn that six of his twelve direct reports were believers. God had carefully placed them there to help this executive accomplish something significant for God's Kingdom.

As you went through the hiring process or the decision process to start a church or ministry, did you have in mind to grow something? When you think about the leaders God has placed in your midst, do they have a growth mindset, or are they content with the size of the church? Isn't most of the Bible about growing? Growing in our faith? Growing our families? Growing groups of Christ-followers? Growing disciples? If you are a church planter who started with a small group of people committed to helping you plant your church, did you use the terms "plant" and "grow" synonymously? You started with nearly nothing and turned it into something bigger, right? No one ever envisions taking a church of a hundred and cultivating it to become a church of sixty, do they? Do these seem like silly questions? They aren't. Did you answer the questions in a way that affirms you are supposed to grow your ministry and church? Keep reading...I'll show you how to activate and deploy church volunteers in chapter 12.

## YOU MIGHT WANT TO CONSIDER...

Assess everyone God has placed in your midst, both inside and outside the church.

- ☑ New Christians in your church who may tell their unchurched friends about Christ and your church or ministry.
- ☑ Those who have been in your church for some time and are prepared to help you grow your church or ministry.
- ☑ Mature Christians in your church who are waiting to be activated and deployed for His Kingdom.

## #3—IS YOUR MINISTRY JUST ABOUT MOVING PEAS ON THE PLATE?

Sadly, many Christians spend a lot of time hopping from one church to another. They may be looking for the "perfect" church to best meet their needs, or perhaps they got their feelings hurt and left the church where they attended. But if most of the new people you get through your doors are detached or de-churched, aren't you just moving peas on the plate? Aren't you taking the body of believers in one area and moving them into another area? Are you really making disciples of all nations by doing that?

It's important to go after the one lost sheep and help people who have been displaced from their church for any reason. But it's also important to go after the multitude of people who have never accepted Christ as Lord and Savior.

Granted, we want to do both. We want to attract the seeking and unchurched as well as any believer wandering around looking for a church home. But where are we expending our energies? What if you looked at it in terms of percentages of time and effort? If 20% percent of your local population is in church on Sundays and 80% of the community is not, what if you spend 80% of your efforts going after the lost in your community and 20% of your time caring for those already in the church?

This concept may not be bad, but the percentages may have thrown you into a tizzy. So what if you spend just 25% of your time going after the lost in your community, 50% of your time caring for those already in the church, and 25% of your time building up the leaders in your church whom God has placed around you to help you grow your church? Do those percentages seem more realistic and doable?

Let's agree on one thing. God doesn't want you to spend 100% of your time caring for only those people inside your church, right?

## YOU MIGHT WANT TO CONSIDER...

- ☑ Spending 25% of your time on reaching the lost in your community.
- ☑ Going after the one lost sheep (the ones who left the church).

### #4—IS YOUR CHURCH PRIMARILY A HOSPITAL FOR THE HURTING OR A HOME FOR THE HEALTHY?

I've watched as the church I've attended for over twenty years grew from 500 people in seats on weekends to 20,000 people. The growth has been tremendous, with multiple church plants and campuses sprouting and growing throughout our city. I heard our senior pastor, Ray Johnston, say that if he could start over, he would have made one significant change. He would have focused a little more on being a home for the healthy instead of a hospital for the hurting.

As our church grew, we started more ministries to help people in desperate need instead of ministries that actively prevented the crisis. For example, with a sky-high divorce rate, it made perfect sense to launch a DivorceCare ministry and one for single adults. Over 40% of the people in our church needed one or both of those ministries. But with a do-over, our senior pastor says he would have also started a Married Life ministry to equip and pour into marriages to prevent divorces in the first place.

Certainly, we are called to help those in need. But might we attract more people to our churches if we think proactively? What if we created ministries that were fun, with an environment for people with similar interests to spend time with each other and encourage one another to get on and stay on the right path, as 1 Thessalonians 5:11 tells us to?

Perhaps people don't like attending church because it's like coming to a hospital (and most people don't like going to the hospital, even if it's just for a visit)! What if our churches were fun, encouraging, and filled with people everyone wanted as friends? What if our churches felt more like a cruise ship that was mostly a home for the healthy, and only a fraction of the people were in sick bay? A ship where, after a little while on board, it felt like everyone was family and navigating rough waters, and day-to-day life was well taken care of.

Wouldn't you like to exist to help lead the vessel known for taking as many people as possible on a journey they had never thought about or didn't know they needed? Plus, you took great care of those already on the vessel and prepared a whole bunch of people to serve on your vessel so you could take even more people. You would serve all sorts of people, as many as God has charged you with.

## YOU MIGHT WANT TO CONSIDER...

☑ Become a "home for the healthy" by creating small groups and ministries that are fun, topic- or special-interest focused, and focusing on the 80% of the population who think they are doing fine (but really aren't).

☑ Create a "hospital for the hurting" by creating small groups and ministries designed to meet the ten felt needs people want to solve (more on that in chapters 11 and 12).

# 3

# ARE YOU CALLED TO GO AND MAKE DISCIPLES?

Many pastors and ministry leaders believe they are supposed to make disciples of only those in their ministry sphere and anyone else who might show up. If that is the case with you, what do you think is the purpose of making disciples? Shouldn't you make disciples so they can, in turn, make other disciples without your help? What are you doing to make them disciples? Perhaps the keyword we should focus on in Matthew 28:19 is GO. The passage doesn't say to wait for people to show up and make them disciples. GO indicates that we need to take action in the same way that MAKE requires action.

We should also consider Matthew 4:19, where Jesus told Peter and Andrew He would teach them to fish for people. Plenty of conjecture comes from this passage about teaching a man to fish instead of feeding him a fish. Should we conclude that we are to be doing more than feeding our congregation on Sunday mornings?

## KEY QUESTIONS FOR THIS CHAPTER

1. Do I actually have to go after the lost?
2. Who will do the discipling?
3. Am I supposed to make disciples by myself?

## #1—DO I ACTUALLY HAVE TO GO AFTER THE LOST?

Is your idea of going after the lost about unlocking the doors to your church (or wherever you do ministry) and putting up an "open" sign? Do you ever talk to God and say, "I'll be open this Sunday, Lord, if you want to send any new people my way," or, "The people who need this ministry will find it"? This may sound direct, but this is what so many church and ministry leaders do. Are you one of them?

Let's say a store opened in your town, and you overheard the owner saying, "I've done my part. I've opened the doors of my business, and now I'm just going to wait for people to come. I'm not going to tell anyone my store exists—no advertising, no social media, no signs or indicators that I am open for business other than the sign out front showing the name of my business." Would you feel confident that the new store will make it and become successful? I know I wouldn't.

When Billy Graham or Luis Palau went to a city, they informed the churches in that city months in advance so they could begin to tell people inside and outside their church that Billy Graham or Luis Palau were coming to town. People inside the church were encouraged to invite their friends and neighbors outside the church to come to hear them.

When the apostle Paul embarked on a mission trip, he would first go to the synagogues in the city and then talk to the multitudes of people in a large public forum.

Wouldn't you agree that Billy Graham, Luis Palau, and the apostle Paul did a lot to reach outside the four walls of the church and go after the lost in the community?

What answer do you get when you pray this prayer: "God, I know you want me to reach the hundreds or thousands of people surrounding my church that don't know you. Do you want me to do something more than just waiting for a visitor to come?" Isn't God looking for a partnership with each of us in which He is calling us to fulfill some responsibility for our part?

My experience is that pastors and ministry leaders often don't know where to start. The first thing to recognize is the chasm between people who grew up in the church and either lead churches or ministries and people who have never been to church or are infrequent visitors. As a leader, you must put yourself in the shoes of the infrequent or first-time visitors, understand what might attract them to church or your ministry, and then present everything in a way they can relate to. At the same time, you must present everything in a way that appeals to those who have been in your church or ministry for years and are called to serve—your volunteers and leaders. We will show you how to do that. Keep reading…

# YOU MIGHT WANT TO CONSIDER...

☑ Do more than unlock your doors on Sunday morning (or the day your ministry meets) to attract first-time and infrequent visitors.

☑ Put yourself in the shoes of someone who has never been to church and imagine what they are feeling and thinking as they contemplate visiting and then attending your church or ministry.

## #2—WHO WILL DO THE DISCIPLING?

Your goal should be to make disciples who make disciples. Your ministry's growth is dependent upon your capacity. The most successful pastors and leaders learn how to model Christ regarding discipleship and ministering to large groups of people. Christ had twelve disciples. Of those twelve, there were three He gave special attention to. Christ also was able to minister to hundreds and thousands of people at one time. Shouldn't we follow this same model?

What if you modeled your ministry after Christ's ministry? You found twelve good people to pour into and minister to regularly, say weekly. These would be your ministry leads, small group leaders, and other leaders in your church. Then, what if you ministered to hundreds or thousands of people once or twice a week on weekends? This would be your church services.

What if you developed a plan and program to disciple the twelve people who reported directly to you (your ministry leads and small group leaders) and deployed the plan so that they could, in turn, deploy it with others within their ministries or small groups? This is a model where disciples make disciples. In this model, one person can come into the church, get discipled, and at some point in the future, become someone who disciples someone else.

This model is scalable. Your church can grow to any size when you have disciples creating disciples. Without this model, your church can only grow based on the time you have available in addition to your weekend services and pouring into your key leaders. The reality of that is apparent around the world…very little discipleship and church growth take place without the disciples-making-disciples model.

The **Church Goals** program is a disciples-making-disciples model. We urge you to deploy a program like the **Church Goals** program that provides content and a roadmap to get there.

## YOU MIGHT WANT TO CONSIDER...

☐ Implement the **Church Goals** program's roadmap for making disciples who make disciples. Here's a graphic of that roadmap:

**START**

**4-WEEK CLASS**
Foundation, framework and strategy of the 12 month program

**FIRST THREE MONTHS - PREPARE**
PREPARE your church for visitors

**SECOND THREE MONTHS - GROW**
GROW your church with a steady stream of new, unchurched visitors

**THIRD THREE MONTHS - EXPAND**
EXPAND - the ministries in your church to meet the needs of your new attendees

**FOURTH THREE MONTHS - SUSTAIN**
SUSTAIN growth by repeating key processes

**YEAR 1 COMPLETION**

## #3—AM I SUPPOSED TO MAKE DISCIPLES BY MYSELF?

After reading the past section, you should know you are not supposed to make disciples by yourself. You want disciples making disciples. I'm really asking a bigger question here. If your overall calling and command as a pastor is to go and make disciples of all nations, are you supposed to do that by yourself? Are you supposed to start your church by yourself? Run the church by yourself? Do all ministry work by yourself? Do every job in the church by yourself?

While those questions may seem absurd, how many pastors try to do it all themselves? Are you one of them? Perhaps you're doing a hybrid of doing it all by yourself. You're doing as much as you can by yourself and giving just a little to a few people.

Have you ever asked yourself why Christ had twelve disciples? Didn't He choose twelve so He could teach them, then activate and deploy them to go out and teach what He taught them? Isn't a disciple someone who assists in spreading the doctrine of another? By definition, if we are to go out and make disciples of all nations, aren't we being commanded to get people to assist us in spreading the doctrine of Jesus Christ? If that's the case, why try to do so much by yourself or with limited assistance?

Are you one of the many pastors or ministry leaders paralyzed by the amount of work you need to do in the limited amount of time you have to do it? God chose you to disciple people. This means He expects you to get people to assist you in spreading the Word. God also expects us to work in partnership with Him. God has likely placed a handful (probably twelve) really gifted people in your vicinity to help you grow your ministry... you just have to identify and ask them, just as Christ did. We'll help you identify, recruit, train, and deploy the people God has placed around you to help expand your church or ministry.

## YOU MIGHT WANT TO CONSIDER...

☑ Think about the twelve people whom God has put around you that you can disciple, who will, in turn, make more disciples.

☑ Employ the **Church Goals** Core Meeting designed to help identify those twelve people.

# ARE YOU PREPARED FOR VISITORS?

### (PREPARE)

# WHY AREN'T PEOPLE COMING TO YOUR CHURCH?

Have you ever wondered why some churches are growing while others are stagnant or declining? Have you considered what causes people to attend church for the first time? When the thought about going to church pops into their head, is it because they thought of it on their own, or could God possibly have whispered that thought?

God created and runs the universe, so we must consider that He might nudge people to visit His Church from time to time. So if people in your community aren't coming to your church, you should probably ask why.

---

### KEY QUESTIONS FOR THIS CHAPTER

1. Is your church ready for God to send new visitors?
2. What experience do you have with being unchurched?
3. Have you ever been a first-time visitor?
4. Why don't people come to church?
5. Does your church have what they are looking for?
6. Do you and the people in your church want your church to grow?

---

## #1—IS YOUR CHURCH READY FOR GOD TO SEND NEW VISITORS?

If God does help orchestrate how people find their way to church, will He send them to your church? Would He send them if He knew they would leave confused, put-off, or cynical about the visit? Wouldn't it be terrible for people to visit a church for the first time and leave saying, "That's what I thought church would be like…I was bored, I didn't understand some of it, and they asked me to do some things I wasn't comfortable doing," and then decided to never go back to church ever again? Wouldn't that be worse than them not visiting your church at all?

Might God be saying, "I can't possibly send your friend or neighbor to your church because they will leave and won't want to come back."

As you're reading these questions, you may be thinking, "Maybe the new visitors to my church would be Christians who have relocated or have left another church and are looking for a new one or would leave another one because they might find my church more appealing." While these situations could be true, isn't our greatest opportunity for the 60% to 90% of people in our communities who don't attend any church? And isn't it possible that even if your new visitors came from a Christian background, they might still find your church boring, confusing, or off-putting?

Matthew 28:19–20 says, "Therefore go and make disciples of all nations, baptizing them in the name of the Father and of the Son and of the Holy Spirit, and teaching them to obey everything I have commanded you. And surely I am with you always, to the very end of the age." There isn't any instruction that says, "Go and make disciples of existing believers." On the contrary, "all the nations" were not full of believers but were primarily unbelievers.

You might be shocked to hear that your church could be boring, confusing, or off-putting to people. Everyone in your church keeps coming, and they seem to like it. Won't everyone like it? It's often difficult for us to look at our own church through the lens of a first-time visitor. Will they understand everything you say? Will they find your sermon riveting and holding their attention for its entire length? Will they be open to participating in your offering or liturgy on Sunday morning? Will they come back after that first visit?

What do you think would happen if you took steps to ensure you weren't boring, that you didn't ask for visitors to participate in things that might make them uncomfortable, and that they fully understood everything you said? Our experience is that people will start visiting and, more importantly, come back. It often feels like God says, "Finally, I can trust you with new visitors… I'll start sending you some."

## YOU MIGHT WANT TO CONSIDER...

- ☐ Take steps to ensure your first-time visitors understand 100% of what is said during a service.
- ☐ Take steps to ensure you are not asking visitors to participate in anything they wouldn't feel comfortable doing or participating in something they aren't familiar with.
- ☐ Take steps to ensure you aren't boring. Make sure you are incorporating all four learning styles into your sermon to make them interesting, relevant, and fun.

☑ Enroll in the **Church Goals** program. The first quarter of the program is dedicated to helping your church get to the position where God says, "Finally, I can send you visitors."

## #2—WHAT EXPERIENCE DO YOU HAVE WITH BEING UNCHURCHED?

Did you grow up in the church, or have you spent many years in the church? My guess is that 99% of the people who read this book have either grown up in the church or attended church for many years. If you grew up in the church, you don't know what it feels like to be unchurched and attend a church service. Maybe you didn't grow up in the church but have attended for years; you may have forgotten what it feels like.

The unchurched come from a different culture. They have different values, missions, and purposes in life. Because of these differences, the unchurched often think they will have to give up all or part of the life they know and like. They may think the church will curtail some or most of the fun they have in their life. Even though this isn't true, it is a big reason why people don't want to come to church.

## YOU MAY WANT TO CONSIDER...

☑ Put yourself in the shoes of a first-time visitor who has never been to church.
☑ Ask God to give you the wisdom and equip you to make the changes necessary for people to start coming to your church.

## #3—HAVE YOU EVER BEEN A FIRST-TIME VISITOR?

If you grew up in the church, it's even more difficult to envision a first-time visit through the lens of someone who has never been in a church or has only been to an Easter, Christmas, or memorial service.

Think back to that first day at a new school. You were likely anxious and had some apprehension. Visiting a church for the first time can cause the same feelings, if not more. God potentially really does exist, and when we go to church, we are going into His realm. This is a difficult concept for anyone to grasp. Add to that the possibility that we haven't lived up to whatever God's standards are, and the anxiety and apprehension get stronger.

You and your regular attendees don't think anything about coming to church on Sunday because you've done it hundreds of times. Those who come to your church for the first time, but have a history of going to church, may have a little anxiety because it's a new experience—a new place, new people. But this is nothing compared to first-time visitors who have never been to church for a weekend service. Yes, they may have visited a church for a wedding or funeral, but that's different.

Here are some questions to consider as you put yourself in the shoes of your first-time visitor:

### WHAT A FIRST-TIME VISITOR MIGHT BE FEELING:

☐ How are they feeling the night before their visit? Anxiety? Worry? Excitement? Apprehension?

☐ What thoughts might they be having? Second thoughts? Concern about the mistakes made in life?

Will the people at the church judge them?

☑ How will they feel as they are driving to your church? Will things go wrong that morning that might prevent them from getting to the church or put them in a bad mood? Will Satan be at work trying to prevent them from coming?
Answer: Definitely.

☑ How will they feel as they are driving to your church? Will they be able to find it? Will they find a parking space? Will it be crowded?

☑ How will they feel in the parking lot, getting out of the car, and walking toward the entrance? Will they know where to go? Are there friendly, smiling faces greeting or directing them?

☑ What will they feel as they meet the first people from your church? What will that experience be like? Will they be recognized as a "new" person and made to feel out of place, or will they be recognized at all? Will they be bombarded with questions like, "Who are you?" "Where are you from?" and "What brought you to church today?"

☑ What are the first words they will hear from the front? (You will read this question a few times because this is important to get right.)

What can you do to ease a first-time visitor's anxiety, concerns, and feelings? If you know the thoughts running through their minds, why not address their concerns? Why not be prepared to put them at ease and make it a wonderful experience instead of anxiety-filled?

Start by putting yourself in their shoes. Trace every step you would take and every thought process you would go through before visiting someplace you are anxious about, like a visit to your new dentist, doctor, or a class at the gym. You can do lots of things to mitigate their anxiety and make it a great experience so they will want to come back, which is the goal.

## YOU MAY WANT TO CONSIDER...

- ☑ Recognize that first-time visitors have some anxiety starting the night before their visit.
- ☐ Give first-time visitors something to talk about and focus on while driving to your church for the first time. You can do this on your website, which we'll talk more about in chapter 8.
- ☑ Strategically place people in your parking lot to greet guests and direct them to a parking space.
- ☑ Prep your greeters, at the entrance to your church and inside the lobby, on how to treat guests. There is a specific way they want to be greeted, which we can help you with.
- ☐ Explain everything in your service that a first-time

visitor may not understand or be comfortable doing (more on this in chapter 8).

☑ Consider the **Church Goals** program. It provides a step-by-step process for each of the above. Go to churchgoals.org for more information.

## #4—WHY DON'T PEOPLE COME TO CHURCH?

Have you ever searched the internet for "why people don't like church"? I would encourage you to do that search. Whether the data is coming from qualified researchers, scientific studies, or personal opinions, the following is a fair representation of why people don't come to church:

*It's boring.*

*They will ask me for money.*

*It's too long.*

*They are hypocrites.*

*All they teach is fire and brimstone.*

*It's confusing.*

*I'll be judged.*

*They'll talk down to me.*

*It's become political.*

*It feels like a cult.*

If you know these are common reasons or excuses, what can you do about them? If you knew that most of your first-time visitors feel one or more of these complaints, what can you do differently so they will leave saying, "That wasn't what I expected"?

People will tell their friends about good experiences after going to someplace new. You can easily start a ground swell of conversation if someone comes to your church and has an unexpectedly great experience. This is how churches and most businesses grow. The opposite is also true.

Unfortunately, some churches are doing things (consciously or not) that fulfill one or more reasons why people don't attend church. Satan is likely sending people to church to confirm their negative expectations so they'll tell others about their bad experiences to keep others from going. Someone may visit just one church in a community and then post that negative experience on social media. By association, people start believing that all churches are that way.

Here's the point: Consider a new type of person coming to church—the unchurched. The unchurched don't think like the people who have been attending forever. God will attract them to the church. Your job is to make it a great experience that overcomes their preconceived notions so they want to return. We will show you how.

## YOU MAY WANT TO CONSIDER...

---

- ☐ Assess every aspect of your church services. Are you committing one or more of the reasons why people don't like church?
- ☐ If yes, take steps to do the opposite.
- ☐ Pray to God for wisdom on becoming the opposite of the list.

---

## #5—DOES YOUR CHURCH HAVE WHAT THEY ARE LOOKING FOR?

Do you know what people are looking for and what might draw them to church? When people go to church, they are looking for three general things: (1) a solution to their problem, (2) community, or (3) to find God. Some people know they are looking for one of those three things and actively search for it. Others don't know they are looking for anything and are guided to you by a friend, some form of outreach from the church, or prompting from the Holy Spirit.

Many churches make the mistake of not knowing what people are looking for. Consequently, they don't make it obvious that they have it. So let's make it obvious. It's possible that God won't send someone specifically looking for a solution to their problem because He knows they won't easily find it at your church; they'll get frustrated and leave.

Keep reading. We will show you how to address each of those three solutions in your church and how to connect a visitor with the particular solution they are seeking.

## #6—DO YOU AND THE PEOPLE IN YOUR CHURCH WANT YOUR CHURCH TO GROW?

Do you think it's possible that people in your church don't want your church to grow? Is it possible that you don't want your church to grow?

Time to get honest. In your head, you may tell yourself that you want your church to grow and reach the lost. But in your heart, you may think, "I like my church the way it is. I like the size of our church. Any more people would upset our church family." If you don't think this way, there are people in your congregation who do. It's very common for people in the church to say they want to reach their lost family members, friends, and neighbors but just not at their own church. It's also very common for those in your church to say, "I like our church the way it is. If we let new people in, they will mess it up." (They either say that to themselves, or it exists in their subconscious.)

Could you be going along with the intent to grow your church and reach the lost but not really making an effort? Some churches give the outward appearance that they want to grow and reach the lost. They do this to appease their denomination or because it sounds like the right thing to do. They often make just enough effort to make it appear that their actions are in sync with their statements, but the results don't materialize.

I was working with a group of churches from one district in a denomination. It appeared that all the churches were implementing every step of the **Church Goals** program, but the results were not the same. One church wasn't growing. After several discussions, it came out that members of the congregation, and eventually the senior pastor, really didn't want their church to grow. They were comfortable and liked the church community the way it was.

It's a good thing we have the Holy Spirit. If you and your congregation are open to letting the Holy Spirit lead a meeting in your church, we are confident you and everyone in this meeting will leave with a revived conviction to reach the lost in your community. You'll hear about this meeting in chapter 8 when we talk about the Core Group meeting.

We've seen so many churches start growing just by making changes to overcome the obstacles presented in this chapter. Churches have consistently grown when they look through the lens of someone who has never been in church and put measures in place to overcome every reason God has for not sending visitors to theirs. And they will continue to grow when they seek to overcome the complaints that the unchurched give for not wanting to attend church. Yours will grow too!

## YOU MAY WANT TO CONSIDER...

☑ Investigate whether you and the people in your church want to reach the lost and grow the church.

☑ Consider holding a Core Group meeting and inviting the Holy Spirit to shape everyone's stance on reaching the lost and growing your church.

Can you see the case I'm building for why people may not be coming to your church? It could be just one of the six questions in this section preventing a steady stream of new visitors.

Are there any questions you have read that resonate? If none, excellent. But it's time to explore why if you aren't seeing a steady stream of new people to your church.

# 5

# WHERE IS YOUR FOCUS?

Did you know that only 8% of the population sets and reaches their goals? [1] This means everyone else is living in default mode. They are letting life pass by without setting and accomplishing their goals. But God doesn't want you to live in the default mode and just respond to life as it presents itself. God wants you to accomplish something significant for His Kingdom with what He has placed in your hands. He has His own goals in mind for you, which requires focus.

If you are waking up each day and just doing what you did the day before or the week or month before, you are living in the default mode. What if you woke up each day with the mindset to accomplish something significant that only you can accomplish because God has equipped you and provided all the resources necessary for you to achieve it? By focusing on the three to four things God tells you to accomplish daily, you will "go and make disciples."

---

[1] "Science Says Only 8 Percent of People Actually Achieve Their Goals," Marcel Schwantes, Inc.com, June 13, 2018, https://www.inc.com/marcel-schwantes/science-says-only-8-percent-of-people-actually-achieve-their-goals-here-are-7-things-they-do-differently.html#:~:text=According%20to%20the%20University%20of,elite%20category%20of%20goal%2Dachievers.

**KEY QUESTIONS FOR THIS CHAPTER**

1. Have you become too comfortable?
2. Have you become distracted from your mission?
3. Are you focusing on what's most important?

## #1—HAVE YOU BECOME TOO COMFORTABLE?

What is the perfect-sized church? Is your church the ideal size because it takes 100% of your time, and you can't imagine it getting bigger because you're already giving it everything you've got? Is it the perfect size because you like the "family feel" it's created? It's manageable and comfortable, and everyone likes it that way.

Have you ever wondered how a pastor runs a church two, three, or ten times larger than your church? Are they working the same hours or two, three, or ten times more? They work the same number of hours each week. It's easy to fill your day with things to do, regardless of size.

Our experience is that people become comfortable with their current daily schedule and tasks and become resistant to change. They often feel things won't get done unless they do it themselves and try to do everything. They are literally too busy to change.

Have you become comfortable as a pastor or ministry leader? Your church is at a size that's manageable for you, and you don't want to change? Maybe you like the size of your church, the size of your congregation, your daily workload, and the general operation of your church. You've become comfortable with your salary, too, and since it keeps coming every few weeks, you just keep doing what you're doing. In other words, your salary is not dependent upon your success. You do not need to grow or accomplish more because you feel well compensated for your current work. Plus, if you grow your church, would you expect more income?

Have you become comfortable because you fit everything you currently do into the hours you want to work each week? Or are you doing all you can each week and can't imagine adding anything more to your plate?

I realize these could be very difficult and pointed questions. Nobody wants to learn they are doing things one way when there is another easier way that produces better results and causes less stress and work. But could it be possible you've become lukewarm? Is it possible you've become complacent?

There are a variety of reasons this happens. Most people do certain things on certain days just because that's what they did last week, last month, last year, etc. They become comfortable with the way things are. But what we are comfortable doing isn't always what God wants us to do, which in this case is to prepare for visitors coming to our church.

Are you living in a default mode? Are you ready to implement changes to produce different results?

## YOU MAY WANT TO CONSIDER...

☐ Begin your day by asking God what He wants you to accomplish that day. What are the top three to four most important things He wants you to do?

☑ Start envisioning what your day would look like if your church doubled in size. How many additional volunteers might you need?

☑ What might it look like to live in the proactive mode instead of the default mode?

## #2—HAVE YOU BECOME DISTRACTED FROM YOUR MISSION?

While I don't give Satan credit for everything that goes sideways or prevents us from accomplishing what God wants us to accomplish, could Satan be involved in taking us away from our mission? We often forget that Satan's ploys are subtle and take place over an extended period. First, he tries to get us just to tolerate sin. Then he moves us to accept the sin. Finally, he wants us to champion the sin. Have you seen this happen in our society over the past five, ten, or twenty years over any issues? I wonder if Satan has learned that if he can put a few poison pills into your church, it will get everyone distracted. Are you getting spun out on cultural issues and how you should respond or handle them? Could those issues keep you from accomplishing what God wants you to accomplish—the very mission He gave you?

Didn't the apostle Paul warn us about people who would come into the church and preach other gospels or try to get us to mix culture into our messages to get us off track? That's what being distracted means—allowing your thoughts and attention to be drawn away from the main mission, which is reaching people for Christ through your church.

Have you neglected your mission to reach people for Christ because you're off-mission? Are you working on something other than the most important things God wants you to work on?

## CONSIDER THESE QUESTIONS:

- ☑ Have you been distracted recently, say the past two years, about something that took place politically?
- ☑ Have you been distracted by racial issues?
- ☑ Have you been distracted by economic issues?
- ☑ Have you been distracted by health issues (like the Covid-19 pandemic)?
- ☑ Have you been distracted by government controls?
- ☑ Are these issues getting in the way of preparing for visitors, making disciples, and growing the church?

If so, you are not alone, but it's time to get back on track. Put on the Kingdom mindset and reset your focus to go and make disciples.

## YOU MIGHT WANT TO CONSIDER...

- ☐ Stop any activity and thoughts relating to the distraction.
- ☐ Rise above anything that distracts you and your church and refocus on your mission, vision, and calling to go out and make disciples.
- ☑ Do only the things necessary to accomplish the mission, which means stop being distracted and resetting your focus.

## #3—ARE YOU FOCUSING ON WHAT'S MOST IMPORTANT?

I'm sure you read that question and said, "Yes, of course, I focus on the most important things every day!" But have you evaluated the most important things to accomplish each day based on the top three to four goals of your church/ministry and your role? Are they in sync?

There are a few steps to determine what your most important priorities are. First, consider your position in the church. If you are the senior pastor, what is the most important role of the senior pastor? Is it to shepherd those you're entrusted with by encouraging and supporting them? If you are the director of a ministry, a volunteer, or an associate pastor, have you determined and defined your role and the most important components of that role?

If you haven't defined your role, responsibility, and authority, it will be difficult to determine the most important things to focus on each day. We tend to do what's most fun and easiest for us naturally, and we reason that it is in line with what we believe to be the direction of the church. But that can get us into trouble if our perceived goals of the church differ from the actual goals. If you don't know how you contribute towards the main goal(s) of the church, you and your church may not be prepared for visitors.

A Core Group meeting will help you determine the most important things for your church to focus on. As guided by the Holy Spirit, your Core Group will determine what those are. I imagine some of them will be centered on preparing for visitors and growth. If you haven't held your Core Group meeting yet, I encourage you to hold one as a beginning step to growing your church.

# YOU MIGHT WANT TO CONSIDER...

- ☑ Start your day by asking God what three to four things He wants you to accomplish today based upon your ministry role (e.g., pastor, volunteer, ministry leader).
- ☐ Hold a Core Group meeting if you haven't done one already. (More in chapter 8.)
- ☑ Determine if there's anything you need to do today based on the outcome of your Core Group meeting.

# 6

# ARE YOU READY FOR VISITORS?

Of course, we're ready for visitors!" says every pastor and member of your church.

As evidenced by what?

"We have empty seats, visitors are always welcome, and we are friendly people," you say.

And if a visitor came to your church, they might agree with your three answers. But would they be comfortable, understand everything, get what they were looking for, and most importantly...want to return? There is a gap in understanding this concept.

The truth is that people aren't just looking for an empty seat, a sign that says they're welcome, and people to treat them well. People need to know they will fit in, find a solution for why they came, and enjoy the experience.

Any restaurant could answer the same question about being prepared for visitors—they have empty seats, a welcome sign, and their staff is friendly. But unless the food is good, served the way it was expected, and for the right price, people won't come back and might even tell their friends about the poor experience (social media).

It will take more than hanging a sign that says everyone is welcome, putting smiles on your faces, and having empty seats to get repeat visitors.

---

## KEY QUESTIONS FOR THIS CHAPTER

1. Is your church ready for visitors?
2. Is your website ready for visitors?
3. Is your church visitor-friendly?
4. Who are you speaking to? (First-timers, relatively new people, the congregation, leaders)
5. Are you teaching in all four learning styles?
6. What do the social media channels say about your church?
7. How are the reviews for your church?

---

## #1—IS YOUR CHURCH READY FOR VISITORS?

Is your church as approachable as the local grocery store, or does it feel like a private club? The only person who can answer this is a first-time visitor to your church.

People are in the habit of going to grocery stores regularly, so they know what to expect. But people don't know what to expect when they walk into a church for the first time, so they will likely want to do some recon.

Consider what emotions or thoughts you think people might have as they approach their first visit to a church or just contemplate a visit to a church. They might think:

*I wonder if God will strike me down when I enter the church because of what I've done in the past.*

*Will the people be friendly?*

*I wonder what they'll think of me when I walk in.*
*"What's he/she doing in church?"*
*"I didn't think I'd ever see you in church."*
*"You don't belong here!"*
*"Do we want to let him/her into our church?"*

*I wonder if it's going to be boring. How long will it be?*

*I wonder if they'll ask me for money.*

*How will I know where to sit? When to stand?*

*They'll judge me.*

*How will I know where to park?*

*Once I park, how will I know where to go?*

*What should I wear?*

For most of us, when we're going to a new place, the first thing we do is go online and do a little (or a lot of) research to check it out. We might ask other people if they have ever been there and their experience. We might look for reviews. We want to know what to expect, right?

How would that go if someone decided to visit your church and run through some or all those steps? Have you thought about how people do their research? What are they looking for? How do they take in the information, and how do they process it?

The first thing someone will likely do is search for your church's name using Google or some other search engine. Will they easily find your church? Will it show up on the first page? If they find it, will it make sense and provide what they are looking for? Whom was the page written for?

We need to make sure your church is ready for visitors by making your church website ready for visitors. We'll talk about that and other ways to make your church visitor-friendly in the next few sections.

## YOU MIGHT WANT TO CONSIDER...

Prepare your website for people researching a visit to your church for the first time. It should be written for three groups of people:

- ☑ People who don't attend your church but who might consider visiting.
- ☑ People who are in your church and want to be informed.
- ☑ People in your church who are leaders and want opportunities to serve.

  Each of those three groups is looking for specific information. The first group is looking to see what you're about and get a feel for whether it would be comfortable for them to attend. Your website will have to provide enough information to get them comfortable visiting, and it must provide enough information to understand how that visit will go and what to expect.

## #2—IS YOUR WEBSITE READY FOR VISITORS?

Websites were initially signs, banners, and replacements for Yellow Page advertisements. They contained only the most basic information about your business or church, such as name, address, hours open, and perhaps upcoming events or something that should be advertised. Today's websites are much different. They provide the basic details I just listed, plus an in-depth look into your business or church. Websites give a history of your organization, tell a story about it, describe what it's like to be part of or associated with your organization, and give a glimpse of what it might be like to attend or do business with you.

Your website was probably designed by Christians with Christian readers in mind…which isn't necessarily bad; you just want to make sure that you also design the site to help people who have never been to church or have attended only sporadically. Let me ask a few questions about your website so you can see if there are any problems or hindrances for a first-time visitor.

1. Does your website contain any language or verbiage written in Christian code or lingo? Do you use words that only Christians use, such as:

| | | |
|---|---|---|
| agape | Christology | praise |
| allegorical | deism | resurrection |
| anoint | epistle | revelation |
| apostle | eucharist | salvation |
| atonement | fellowship | secular |
| baptism | fruit (of the Spirit) | Omni-(anything) |
| bishop | Gospel | stewardship |
| Calvin(ism) | incarnation | theology |
| Catechism | justification | tribulation |
| confession | liturgy | Trinity |
| consecrate | Luther | worship |
| covenant | Messiah | sin (sinful) |

You can't assume everyone knows what all the words mean, including the ones on the list, and that they define them the way you would.

2. Does your website contain what they are looking for?

☐ Information for a first-time visit. What can they expect?

☐ Directions to the church

☐ Service times, along with descriptions, if different service times offer different experiences

☐ Parking information

☐ A map of your church, so people know where to go once they arrive

☐ What to wear

☐ What to do with their children if they bring them

☐ Solutions to the felt need that brought them to your church website and, by extension, potentially to your church on Sunday morning. For example, if someone is looking for a better group of friends for their wayward teenager, would they find you have that solution in your Youth Group?

3. Does your website have high-quality recordings of previous services?

☑ People will want to see what a service is like at your church.

☑ People will go to great lengths to see if you or someone has recorded a service and posted it online — even on websites other than your church's

☐ Are online recordings edited well?
- Not too long (i.e., not too boring)
- No gaps or lulls
- Good audio
- Everything said is understandable and comprehendible.

4. Does your website convey personal safety?

☐ If visitors bring their children, their children's safety is vital. Will they glean that from your website?

☐ What does your website say for adults concerned about personal health issues?

☐ People provide a measure of safety. Do you have photos of people that are part of your church who help provide a safe environment, such as photos of your Sunday school teachers?

5. Speaking of photos…does your website have images that depict your staff/volunteers and what it will be like at your church? Visitors want to see if everyone looks normal and if the people in your church look like people they would want to hang out with.

☑ Photos of people having fun talking to each other?

☑ Photos of children having fun in Sunday school?

☑ Photos of your staff and congregation?

☑ Photos of people in the service?

☑ Photos of events showing the kinds of things your church gets involved in?

6. Does your website provide information about what you believe and your church's values?

☑ Do you have a statement of faith saying what your church believes?

☑ If your church is missional-oriented, is the mission described on your website?

☑ Is your church's mission something a person would be interested in if they have never been to church? Reaching people for Christ is a great mission, but it isn't necessarily understood or embraced by someone who hasn't been to church. Better missions will be outlined in chapter 11.

7. Is your website designed and written so people can find you?

☑ If someone types "church near me" and is within a few miles of your location, does your church show up on the first page and near the top?

☑ Is your church registered with Google Business? If not, it won't likely show up or provide much information about your church. I'll explain how to do this in chapter 10.

☑ Have your web pages been structured to comply with how search engines qualify data? If not, or you don't understand the question, no problem—chapter 10.

☑ Have your web pages been designed and written so that web crawlers categorize the most pertinent information about your church and rank it highly? If not, or you don't understand the question, that's okay—I'll explain it in chapter 10, too.

☑ Is your website mobile-friendly, meaning it shows well on a mobile device?

☑ Is your website engaging and somewhat fun?

☑ Will people enjoy visiting and using your website?

## YOU MIGHT WANT TO CONSIDER...

☑ Redesign your website to meet the expectations a visitor would have relating to questions 1–7 above.

☑ If that task seems daunting, don't worry. The **Church Goals** annual program will help you deploy a new website to achieve the above.

## #3—IS YOUR CHURCH VISITOR-FRIENDLY?

Nearly every pastor I've talked with has said their church is "visitor friendly." Almost every church I've visited had very friendly people. And yet, nearly every church I've visited has not been "visitor friendly."

The definition of "visitor friendly" that we will use here is as follows:

*A visitor can come to your church for the first time*
*and find every aspect of the experience enjoyable*
*and understandable to the extent that they want to return.*

It takes a deliberate process to make your church visitor-friendly, where most first-time visitors will enjoy your church and want to come again. Consider these questions:

- ☑ As they get close to your church, does it become easier to find your church?
- ☑ Will guests know where to park for their first visit?
- ☑ Is it clear where they should go after they park their car?
- ☑ Who will greet these first-time visitors, and what should the greeters say?
- ☑ How will a greeter's first words impact the visitors?
- ☑ How should the members of your church treat these visitors? What should they say to them, if anything?
- ☑ What are the first words someone will hear during their visit? Will they be comprehendible?

☐ Will they understand every word you say throughout your message (think Christian lingo discussed earlier)?

☐ Are there any responsive readings or rituals your visitor may not understand?

☑ Will people in the room be doing things that might be confusing, such as greeting each other with specific phrases, praying, raising their hands during worship, speaking in tongues, shouting out during your message, and so forth?

☐ Will you single out your visitors in a way that makes them uncomfortable, like having them stand up, raise their hand, or direct them to a certain area after the service?

☐ Are the next steps for visitors clear?

☑ Have you smothered your first-time visitors in any way or done something that might feel icky to them?

If you've already considered most of these questions and have steps in place for each answer, you probably have a visitor-friendly church. If you don't, you will need to address the questions above and put a solution in place for each one. We can help you do that.

## #4—WHO ARE YOU SPEAKING TO?

I heard John Maxwell describe heaven as a cartoon. He described how a toddler could enjoy the cartoon and be completely enthralled with the vibrant colors, animation, music, and action. This would be analogous to someone who just recently became a Christian, died, went to Heaven shortly after, and thoroughly enjoyed how amazing being in Heaven was.

Then he described the parents of the toddler. They were watching the cartoon, and in addition to enjoying everything the toddler was enjoying, they were also enjoying the dialog and humor built into it. This was analogous to those who had been in the church for several years and understood much of what was taking place in Heaven as it related to the Bible they had read throughout the years. They were part of the congregation of the church.

Then he described the grandparents of the toddler who were watching the cartoon as well. They, too, enjoyed everything their grandchild and son and daughter-in-law were enjoying, but they enjoyed a different perspective of the cartoon. They were intrigued by how the cartoon had deeper meanings and nuances. Perhaps they saw how it fit into an overall story and plan for the cartoon. Similarly, there will be those who get to Heaven whom God deployed to serve in His Kingdom as leaders while on the earth. They understood more than what was being taught to the core congregation and much more than the first-time visitors could comprehend.

The point is this: Heaven is going to be amazing for the person who accepted Christ just a few days before they died; it's going to be amazing for the person who has spent years in church but hasn't moved into a leadership role; it's going to be amazing for those whom God has called to serve in His Church.

When someone leaves your church this weekend, will it be equally amazing for those same groups (i.e., the brand new, the congregation, and the leaders)? If God's Kingdom comes and His will is done on Earth as it is in Heaven, will everyone leave your church each weekend saying it was amazing and completely understandable? Shouldn't people who are seeing a church service for the first time enjoy it as much as the toddler who sees a cartoon for the first time? Shouldn't the person who has been a member of your congregation for some time leave saying, "That was a great message, so applicable to what's going on in my life today"? And shouldn't a person who is a volunteer or leader in your church, whom God has called to serve in your midst and help you grow your church or ministry, leave on Sunday morning saying, "Amazing sermon, so applicable to how I serve in God's Kingdom and lead others"? Are your first-time visitors, regular congregation members, and leaders giving those responses as they leave each weekend?

If you are like most pastors, you are likely delivering a message that resonates with the middle group—those who have been part of your congregation for some time. But you've likely missed connecting with the first-time visitors and the leaders in your church. It was too deep or too many words or contained elements a first-time visitor wouldn't understand, and it was too shallow and too much of what your leaders had already heard before in previous years in the church. You could be at risk of losing the leaders God has put in your midst and the person who just came to your church for the first time.

Now think back to the question in chapter 1: "Is God willing to send first-time visitors to your church?" Probably not if there's a good chance they will leave confused and put off by your message.

# YOU MIGHT WANT TO CONSIDER...

- ☑ Once your sermon is developed, add explanations and illustrations so the first-time visitor can understand and relate to it.
- ☑ Consider a separate message for your key leaders and volunteers that adds to your original sermon. Get with them before the service (as they are gathering to serve), midweek, or in a video to deliver this "bonus content" for leaders.

## #5—ARE YOU TEACHING IN ALL FOUR LEARNING STYLES?

Do you know your primary learning style? Did you know that you likely teach in your primary learning style? The four learning styles are visual (seeing), auditory (hearing), reading and writing (thinking), and kinesthetic (doing). Each of us has a preferred learning method, our primary learning style, and a minor learning style (the second preferred way we learn). Pastors will teach in their primary learning style with a little of their minor learning style mixed in. They typically leave out the other two learning styles. If you aren't incorporating all four learning styles, you are likely not connecting with half or more of your audience.

Most pastors think they are great teachers and preachers because a few people come up to them after the service every week and tell them how great the message was and how it was so perfect for them. Chances are, the message was preached in the primary learning style of those who came forward to say how great the message was. It's possible that 75% of the room could be leaving saying, "It was okay; it didn't really resonate with me."

The solution to teaching in all four learning styles is very simple and easy to incorporate. First, develop your sermon as you have since you started preaching. Next, list the four learning styles at the top of your first page. Now go through your sermon and incorporate something for each of the three remaining learning styles in each of the segments or sections of your sermon. I say three because it's already written in one of the learning styles—the one you like to teach in.

I'll go into more detail about the learning styles in chapter 8.

## #6—WHAT DO THE SOCIAL MEDIA CHANNELS SAY ABOUT YOUR CHURCH?

Did you know there are over eighty social media sites? Most people only think of a few larger ones, such as Facebook, Instagram, Pinterest, and LinkedIn, but there are seventy-six other platforms. Are you getting spun out by what people are saying on these sites about your church, or are you spending too much time looking at these sites and wondering what's going on?

Do a quick search on how many people look at social media daily and how much time they spend on those sites. The numbers are staggering. I won't quote any one source because any data is outdated almost immediately. Suffice it to say that billions of people worldwide use social media, and many spend a couple of hours on those sites daily. No matter the real numbers, people spend a lot of time on social media.

Unfortunately, social media allows people to provide content, and most of it isn't something you can control. It's like a billboard. Someone can create a billboard that says your church is horrible, and hundreds or thousands of people might come across it and often believe it.

The opposite is true, too. You can create a billboard on social media that hundreds or thousands of people will see, telling people your church is great, and so are you.

Based on the previous two paragraphs, can you see that social media has to be addressed? If someone says something negative about you or your church, you need to respond and set the record straight or at least respond if the person had a good point but was still negative about you or your church.

If someone is thinking about visiting your church, they are likely checking social media to see what people say about it. They are also checking your social media sites (if you have them) to see what they say about your church.

Here are some important questions you should be asking about your social media presence:

- ☑ Does your church have a social media presence?
- ☑ On which sites do you have a presence, and on which sites should you have a presence?
- ☑ Is your social media set up so people looking for a church, or your church specifically, will find it on social media?
- ☑ Are your social media sites visitor friendly? (Use the same criteria discussed in the previous website section.)

☐ Do you have someone in your church (a volunteer or staff member) who manages your social media?

☐ Do you have a proactive social media mindset (like telling people what's going on at your church), or do you have a reactive mindset (responding when you hear something good or bad)?

☐ Do you use any tools to alert you when someone posts something positive or negative about you or your church…so you can manage responses?

☐ Have you insulated yourself from social media so you don't get too spun out by what people say about you and your church?

Social media can be a good thing and a bad thing. We've encountered many pastors who have bad experiences with social media by either wasting too much time listening to the negative said about them and their church or thinking social media alone will provide a steady stream of new visitors to their church.

## #7—HOW ARE THE REVIEWS FOR YOUR CHURCH?

Do you look for reviews on products, services, or experiences you consider buying or taking? If you look for a restaurant you're considering visiting, or when traveling, do you check out the reviews for potential restaurants? It's almost standard that people look for reviews on everything they are considering these days.

What are people saying about your church? What reviews are you getting? They probably exist, and if they don't, that says something, too. But social media needs to be managed! You can't just have a Facebook or Instagram account and hope it goes okay. Social media needs daily interaction to be effective. You'll hear about how we recommend doing this in chapter 10.

## YOU MIGHT WANT TO CONSIDER...

☑ Recognize that social media is just one tool in the toolbox that should inform people about your church and can convey positive experiences associated with your church.

☑ Find one person in your church to hire or to be a volunteer whose job it is to manage all social media for the church.

☑ The **Church Goals** program helps equip and train volunteers or staff on social media management.

# 7

# IS YOUR CHURCH RELEVANT?

A lot is happening in the world today that has caused people to become fearful, depressed, and discouraged. It's true that church attendance surges whenever there has been a major disaster or worldwide dilemma. When people become fearful, many look to see if the Church can provide comfort and a solution. But have you done a good job letting people know the Church (God) has the solution? Or are you just opening your doors on Sunday morning, turning on the "open" sign, and allowing people to come in? If that's the case, your church will only see a trickle of visitors come when a disaster occurs, which is nothing compared to the surge in searches on the internet of people looking for answers and solutions.

As the Church, shouldn't we be the ones people turn to for answers? Is your church addressing relevant issues in a timely manner in a way people will feel encouraged? Do you understand people's needs, and can you speak to those needs in your ministries and message? Relevancy means appropriate to the current time, period, or circumstances. Let's find out how to stay current while staying on mission.

## KEY QUESTIONS FOR THIS CHAPTER

1. What do people want and need?
2. Are you preaching on relevant issues?
3. Are you addressing felt needs in the sermon?
4. Where do timing and relevance converge?

## #1—WHAT DO PEOPLE WANT AND NEED?

People come to church looking for three basic things:

1. They come for community and to be educated, inspired, and encouraged.
2. They go because they have a felt need in their life.
3. They come because of the things that are happening around them and in the world that have them concerned.

Most Christians, who are not in a difficult season of life, come for reason number one. The church is a place for them to connect with others like them, learn more about the Bible, and apply what they've learned. A few unchurched people will come if they are introduced to the community that exists in the church and invited to an event or a service on Sunday. There are plenty of people who don't have a specific need to go to church but will be attracted to it because of the community it creates. Because God created us to be in relationships (with Him and others), we all desire to be in a community of some kind. Churches can create that community by creating key ministries you'll hear about in chapter 12 based on the areas of interest in their life.

That said, the greatest opportunity exists for those looking to solve a felt need. If you look at what people are searching for on the internet relating to their personal needs, they are looking to solve one or more of these ten felt needs:

1. A relationship problem (marriage, divorce, separation, estrangement)
2. Looking to get into a relationship (they are single)
3. An issue with their children or teenagers
4. A financial issue
5. An addiction issue (drugs, alcohol, pornography)
6. A problem at work
7. A health problem
8. They are grieving (recently lost someone).
9. They have a special interest (hobby, sport, or activity) and are looking for that community.
10. They are looking for encouragement and hope (they are fearful, depressed, and discouraged).

People want solutions relating to something on the list. The Church as a whole has the solution to every one of those needs. But if they come to your church and it's not obvious that you have the solution, you will lose them. Do you have what they are looking for—community, education, inspiration, and encouragement? Does your church address their felt needs?

## #2—ARE YOU PREACHING ON RELEVANT ISSUES?

Whatever you are preaching this weekend, will it be relevant to the people listening? Perhaps more importantly, will they leave saying, "That message was so important for me to hear based on what's happening in the world and my life right now"? Making your messages relevant to what people are dealing with and experiencing in life right now is vital.

How do you decide what you're going to preach each weekend? Is it established at the denomination level or by a committee? Will you preach on a topic, a book in the Bible, or a specific passage? Are you preaching what you believe your congregation needs to hear or what they want to hear?

Many pastors have a mindset that people need to hear the word of God, so whatever they preach will be good for them—they need to hear it. While everyone might agree with this as a general statement, doesn't the Bible tell us that not everyone is ready to hear everything you could preach? First Corinthians 3:1 tells us, "Brothers and sisters, I could not address you as people who live by the Spirit but as people who are still worldly—mere infants in Christ. I gave you milk, not solid food, for you were not yet ready for it. Indeed, you are still not ready."

There are two issues here. You think you know what people need to hear, but they have issues or problems they are trying to solve and hope the Church has the solution.

What if you went to the grocery store tomorrow? As you walked in, you were handed a bag of groceries, and the grocer said, "I know you came here for food today. Here is the food you need." Wouldn't you instantly say, "How do you know what I need? I want to pick out what I want, not what you think I need. Your bag isn't relevant to me." This is often what we are doing in the church. People are walking in with needs, but we are telling them what we want to tell them instead of what they want to hear, and they leave saying, "That message wasn't meant for me."

Learn what people want to hear—based on their felt needs, major events that are relevant to them, etc.—and design your message around that. If your sermon topics are determined by someone other than yourself, find a way to make the sermon relevant to what people want to hear.

We also know that one of the reasons why people don't want to go to church is that they won't find the message relevant. What good does it do to preach a message people don't want to hear?

## YOU MIGHT WANT TO CONSIDER...

☐ One of the goals of the **Church Goals** program is to help pastors become lifelong learners of their craft and to be effective communicators. To that end, we provide resources to help pastors continue to hone their communication skills. Make it your passion to become a better communicator. Let us coach you in this area. Even those at the top of their game have coaches.

### #3—ARE YOU ADDRESSING FELT NEEDS IN THE SERMON?

If you know that a third of the people coming to your church on Sunday are hurting and need help, wouldn't you want to help them? And if you have a pretty good idea of what they are hurting from, wouldn't you want to give them something to ease their pain, fear, or concern?

If you know a third of your church comes because they want to be in a community with like-minded people and others with similar interests, wouldn't you want to help them meet that need?

Still, others come because they want to be encouraged and inspired. They want to live according to God's will, or they want to be encouraged about their future. You can help them with that too.

You will become relevant when you address people's pain, longing for community, or need for encouragement each week. You simply must weave into your sermon that your church has solutions to help them. If you have the list in front of you when you're preparing your sermon, you can weave in comments like this:

> *"Some of you here this morning are concerned about health issues (like Covid-19) and might even be fearful about your future...."*

> *"Is anyone here this morning concerned about their finances? I know I am from time to time...."*

> *"If you are raising a child or teenager, you know it can be really challenging at times...."*

> *"Have you ever wondered how to make your hobby (or special interest) into a positive thing that your wife or husband will encourage you to do more often...like playing golf or dirt bike riding...?"*

But don't leave it there. Follow up with something like,

> *"I want to give you some hope about your future..."*

If you know what they are looking for and say that you have something that might provide a solution, they will be interested and see if it fits their needs. Don't forget, we have the ultimate solution—God. While we are doing our part to introduce them to the solution by planting seeds and watering them, God is the only one who can make the seeds grow. God will be working on them from the inside, telling them they need to be there, that the solution you are presenting is good, and that they have come to the right place.

## YOU MIGHT WANT TO CONSIDER...

☐ Complete your sermon and then go back and insert several phrases like those above throughout the message, followed by how your church or ministry has the solution to their need or can help them achieve what they are hoping to achieve.

### #4—WHERE DO TIMING AND RELEVANCE CONVERGE?

We've talked about the differing felt needs of your churchgoers and different reasons why they've decided to attend, but what about the differences in their spiritual journeys? How do you accommodate an audience that has people with varying levels of knowledge regarding the Bible?

For example, how do you handle the first-time visitor who shows up at your church in the middle of your ten-week series on Daniel? Everyone in the church knows what's going on. Still, the first-time visitor walks in when you're explaining the difference in the prophecies between chapters 7 and 8 in Daniel and giving the viewpoints from the Preterists, the Futurists, and the Historicists. There's a good chance they walk away saying, "I didn't understand half the words that were being used, and I didn't find the answer to the problem or need that brought me to the church." You can see we have possible relevance issues and a timing issue.

The best way to address something like this is by explaining the terms you are using, what's happening in history and how it might be similar to things we are experiencing today. Couldn't you point out that throughout history, there have always been the same issues we are dealing with today? Haven't there always been relationship issues between people, some that caused wars, like when the Medo-Persian Empire overtook the Babylonian Empire described in Daniel 7 and 8? Do you think the people in Babylon and other parts of the world were fearful about what was happening between the different empires and kingdoms of the world? Do you think there were relationship issues during the time of Daniel? People still got drunk; sex was still an issue that got people messed up; people still raised children that turned into teenagers who caused their parents grief; greed was still an issue...basically, every challenge we have today took place throughout history. Some of those issues were taking place right here in Daniel 7 and 8.

You could make the case that 100 years from now, people will be looking back and saying, "There was a lot of strife in the 2020s. There was a division between Democrats and Republicans, Conservatives and Liberals, blacks and whites, genders, and Russians and Ukrainians." This is like the strife between the people in Daniel 7 and 8, who were called Medo-Persians and Babylonians. And the Preterists, Futurists, and Historicists are just people who read history and put a label on what kind of history it is and whether their thinking aligns with one of them or not. It's no different than how we look at and label things today. During your sermon, you can point out your church's solutions and how successful you are at meeting the felt need.

Ultimately, you must give people two things: (1) confidence that your church has a solution that will work for their struggles and needs, and (2) something to think about—to walk away feeling more encouraged and a little more knowledgeable about their place in the world.

## YOU MIGHT WANT TO CONSIDER...

- ☐ No matter what you preach or where you are in the Bible, provide context and explain terms that make it relevant to the audience today.
- ☐ To be relevant, no matter what you preach, you must convey that you are aware of the world's issues today, what people are struggling with, and that your church has a solution that will work. They will be encouraged and filled with hope as a result.
- ☐ The **Church Goals** program can help you provide a solution to every felt need that brings people to your church, including those already in your church.

# 8

# WHAT WILL IT TAKE TO PREPARE FOR VISITORS?

Did you know that the difference in scores over the course of a season between the highest-paid professional golfers (> $1 million/year) and those making much less (< $100,000 /year) is less than one stroke on average per round? There's just a fraction of a percent difference.

The difference between your church growing versus remaining stagnant or in decline could be just some fractional changes in what you do and how you operate. We've heard so many pastors tell us that they have done over 90% of the things outlined in this book and the **Church Goals** program, but when they did the final few things, they started growing. They went from surviving to thriving—seeing God's Kingdom expand because people were coming to Christ.

Like those professional golfers at the top of their game, the churches that grew did a little more preparation. They did a few more things than they did before they became leaders.

**KEY QUESTIONS FOR THIS CHAPTER**

1. How will you get everyone on board, including yourself?
2. Will a visitor understand what's going on?
3. Will you need to become a better preacher?
4. Will you need to become a better leader?

## #1—HOW WILL YOU GET EVERYONE ON BOARD, INCLUDING YOURSELF?

Have you ever considered that each person in the church has their perception of what the church's goals should be and how to reach them? Or maybe they don't even realize the benefit of creating goals. The bottom line is that you must get your congregation on the same page with what God wants for your church. Right now, there's a good chance everyone in your church, including you, is more focused on what they want for the church, not necessarily what *God* wants for His church.

God has "placed" people around you in your church to help you achieve His mission for your church. A Core Group can help get everyone on the same page and create goals/steps in line with what God wants. The core is everyone who has been placed in your church to help you grow it.

To get what God wants, we recommend holding what we call a "Core Group meeting" and enlisting the help of the Holy Spirit. As it sounds, the Core Group meeting is a meeting of your church's core and one of the most important tools you could deploy in your church. It is flawless at getting everyone in a church on the same page regarding the mission, vision, direction, and necessary action steps.

The Core Group meeting is a gathering of leaders, key volunteers, potential leaders, long-time attendees, representatives from every age group, and anyone else who cares about the direction of your church. The goal is to get 25% to 50% of your church in a room for a meeting to ask what God wants you and all those in attendance to do with His church. Our experience is when you ask God that question...He will tell you. But you must ask a particular set of questions in a particular order, or the meeting becomes about the same arguments regarding the direction of your church you've had for years.

What would happen if you held a meeting and started it by telling the story from chapter 2 about Christ's return and making your church His home base, and then you asked everyone these four questions?

1. What do we like about our church that others might like too?
2. Who is God calling us to go after in our community?
3. How might we go after them?
4. Where is God calling each person at the Core Group meeting to serve? Who is God calling them to go after, and how will they do it?

If you ask everyone at your Core Group meeting these questions and only these questions, and you all agree on the answers, you will have everyone on the same page about the mission, vision, and direction of your church, as well as a pathway to get there. Regularly gathering the "core" people whom God has placed in your midst to accomplish His mission and vision for your church is one of the most important things you can do. We recommend gathering this group at least four times yearly (six to eight times is better).

The Core Group meeting is one of the first tools deployed in the **Church Goals** program. We provide a step-by-step outline and instructions for establishing your first Core Group meeting and follow-up meetings. In the Core Group meeting, you will get everyone on board with what God is calling your church to accomplish with what He's put in your hands. We have yet to see a Core Group meeting deployed where the church isn't unified in its direction, and everyone isn't excited about the future of their church, along with the plan to get there—including the senior pastor.

The Core Group meeting gets everyone in your church open to and excited about reaching people outside your church for Christ. Once the congregation is open to unchurched people coming to your church, you must prepare for visitors.

## YOU MIGHT WANT TO CONSIDER...

- ☑ Hold a Core Group meeting as soon as possible.
- ☑ Ask only the four questions outlined in this section (don't waiver on this).

### #2—WILL A VISITOR UNDERSTAND WHAT'S GOING ON?

In chapter 6, we asked some questions a first-time visitor might be thinking. Now we need to prepare so a visitor won't come to your church only to leave saying it was boring, confusing, and uncomfortable. The first thing you'll need to do is explain everything (don't worry, we'll walk you through it).

If you record your weekend services, I want you to go back and watch your last weekend's service through the eyes of someone who has never been to church before. Would they understand everything you said, right from the first words to the last word? Did you perform any ritual or liturgy they may not understand? Did you ask them to give a response or repeat something they may not know how to respond to or have never done before? Did you ask them to participate in something that might have made them uncomfortable? How is the atmosphere in the service? Energetic? Dull? Do you have people raising their hands during worship or speaking in tongues? Perhaps there are things in your church that represent something symbolic, or something church members do to reflect their worship, but if a visitor came in and saw people doing it, they wouldn't understand...and it might make them uncomfortable.

Everything you do as a pastor or ministry leader is normal and natural for you and the people in your church because you've done them forever. But it's not normal and natural for the first-time visitor. We don't realize it, but church members speak in code and use a foreign language. We use terms that are not used outside the church and perform rituals that only people inside the church understand. Visitors will be lost, confused, put off, and potentially resistant to returning. Churches are foreign places with their own culture. We should be happy to bring outsiders in and make them feel comfortable and welcomed, and we should be excited about sharing our culture and its significance with them. They will be interested.

The good news is that what can be boring, confusing, and off-putting can become interesting and attractive if you explain it to them. We've learned that if you take just a few minutes to unpack the things that an "outsider" might not understand, they will be intrigued. We've seen the most liturgical elements within a church become "pretty cool" once they were explained. Think of this as visiting a foreign country and being invited to an event every week in that country. If the event contained significant cultural components, wouldn't you want to know the significance of those components and how and why they did them? If they invited you to participate in the event, wouldn't you want to know what you were participating in and what it meant? If it sounded interesting and you sensed it was beneficial to participate, wouldn't you want to learn how to engage and do it in a way that didn't make you look awkward or stand out as an outsider?

## OPENING LINES

Start right at the beginning. If the first words spoken in church demand a response, tell everyone how to respond and explain why it has a specific response. If you ask people to "stand up and worship," they will likely understand "stand up" but won't understand worship. Worship who? How do we worship? You might think they will catch on quickly when everyone starts singing, but they will still be puzzled about whom they are standing to worship. Don't assume they understand you are worshipping God. Even if you say, "Let's stand up and worship God," provide just a little more explanation. You could say, "Welcome to (your church); we're glad you're here. We start our services by singing songs to God; we call them praise and worship songs. Please join us."

If the first words spoken demand a response, tell everyone what you're going to say, why you say it, and what the response is. For example, if it's Easter and you open with "He is risen" without an explanation, and everyone around the first-time visitor says, "He is risen indeed," that visitor instantly feels foolish and like an outsider because everyone knows the answer except them. Instead, your first words could be, "Good morning and Happy Easter. Easter celebrates the resurrection of Jesus Christ.

Because this is a celebration, we greet each other on Easter by saying, 'He is risen,' and we respond to that by saying, 'He is risen indeed.'" Then say, "He is risen…" and listen to their response.

## ANNOUNCEMENTS AND BULLETINS

If you make announcements, be careful not to make it all about the insiders of the church. Don't call people out by name or allow members of the congregation to announce they are selling their car or that sister Betty had her gallbladder removed, and we all need to pray for her. Make announcements about the important things everyone needs to know to build excitement and community within the church. We also recommend keeping them short and concise. While every ministry and even some individuals would like to have something announced, there isn't time, and it will become boring to the first-time visitor…and many others in your church. Limit your announcements to the two to three most important things that everyone must know about—the rest can be placed in a bulletin and on the website.

## RITUALS AND LITURGY

The first words or the first liturgical element that occurs in your church must be explained if they are not 100% commonly used outside the church. If your church starts with any ritual, briefly explain what you will do. God won't mind that you're explaining it, and it might even be a nice reminder for some people in your congregation that may have forgotten why you do it. For example, some churches have prayer candles. One candle is always lit, and church members can come to the candle area and light another candle for prayer. There's a lot of symbolism associated with how the candles are laid out. What if you put a small sign on these kinds of things that briefly describe the item, how it's used, and what it represents?

Think of a small explanation sign at a museum attached to the artifact it's associated with.

## SPECIFIC WORD CHOICES

Do you use words in your sermon that new visitors won't understand? Most pastors do. Many pastors like to use Greek and Hebrew terms throughout their sermons. While it's nice to know the pastor did a thorough study while prepping for the sermon, stating the Greek or Hebrew terms seldom adds to the understanding or importance of the passage. We recommend using Greek and Hebrew sparingly and only when it's relevant to conveying the meaning of a certain word or phrase that can't be explained any other way.

In addition to Greek and Hebrew, pastors use words that only people who have studied Christianity and the Bible would understand. As I discussed in chapter 6, any words that a person in the grocery store wouldn't understand needs to be defined and explained.

Here's that list again:

| | | | |
|---|---|---|---|
| agape | confession | Gospel | salvation |
| allegorical | consecrate | incarnation | secular |
| anoint | covenant | justification | Omni-(anything) |
| apostle | Christology | liturgy | stewardship |
| atonement | deism | Luther | theology |
| baptism | epistle | Messiah | tribulation |
| bishop | eucharist | praise | Trinity |
| Calvin(ism) | fellowship | resurrection | worship |
| Catechism | fruit (of the Spirit) | revelation | sin (sinful) |

These are presented to give you an idea of the types of words often used in a sermon that the unchurched person wouldn't understand. Start to train yourself to listen to the words you are preaching and stop to explain a word when necessary so your guests understand it.

## COLLECTION OF MONEY

While most churches are eager to collect money from anyone who comes to their church, remember that being asked for money is one of the top three to four reasons people give for not wanting to go to church. If we know it puts people off, let's just let them off the hook. Doesn't God want a cheerful giver who is a follower of Christ? Taking money from people who do not follow Christ is like being invited to hear someone speak on a subject they thought you might find interesting and then being asked to support that cause whether you believed in the cause or not. Your guests will find it refreshing to hear, "We are about to take our offering this morning. This offering is for those who call (your church) home and support its ministries. If you are here for the first time, please let the offering bucket pass by. You are our guest, and we are just glad you are here." Make sure to explain this clearly.

## TAKING COMMUNION

If your church takes communion, explain it, why you do it, and to whom it applies. Communion is a sacrament that should be explained. The concept of Christ dying for our sins may not be understood or accepted for some time by the unchurched. Whether your church invites the participation of everyone in attendance to take communion or only those who have accepted Christ as Lord and Savior, you must explain what communion is and provide an "out" if someone isn't comfortable participating. You can simply say, "If you have not yet accepted Christ as

Lord and Savior, we invite you to watch this element of our service instead of participating in it. It will have much greater meaning after you come to know Jesus Christ as Lord and Savior," or "If you are fairly new to the church and are not comfortable participating, that's okay. You're welcome just to observe."

Remember, your goal is to have visitors understand everything they hear, be comfortable with everything they experience, and want to return. If you see anything that might make a first-time visitor uncomfortable or not understand, find a way to explain its purpose, history, and significance. It will also serve as a reminder to those already in the church and help them teach it to visitors they bring to the church. Our experience is that it takes about three months for a church to become truly "visitor friendly" while not detracting from its DNA, liturgy, or becoming off-putting to its own congregation. The **Church Goals** program helps churches get to the point where they can hear God say, "Finally, I can send visitors to your church and know they won't be bored, confused, or asked to do something they aren't comfortable doing."

## YOU MIGHT WANT TO CONSIDER...

- ☑ Go back to the beginning of your service and look at it from a first-time visitor's point of view.
- ☑ Work out how to explain everything simply in a way that is not off-putting or repetitive.
- ☑ Don't worry; we can help!

## #3—WILL YOU NEED TO BECOME A BETTER PREACHER?

The short answer is…YES! Preparing for visitors means becoming a better preacher and teacher. We hope you make it your lifelong passion and goal to become a better communicator. After all, that is your profession. The people who are the best at their professions practice regularly and always seek to improve. Most have coaches. Have you ever wondered why professional athletes at the top of their game still have coaches? Because they want to strive to improve and remain at the top of their game. The same is true for communicators. The best communicators are always looking for ways to communicate better. It's important to become a lifelong learner of your craft.

Here's why you need to become a better preacher. You likely get a few people who come up to you after every sermon and tell you how wonderful it was and how it touched them so deeply or spiritually. But that was only a few people. How did everyone else feel about your message? Unless you teach in all four learning styles (as described in chapter 6), people will leave bored and confused.

That brings up the next reason. Don't be boring. If boring is listed among the top three reasons people don't like going to church, then pastors must be boring. That can be fixed. In addition to teaching in all four learning styles, there are concepts and strategies to build into your speaking game to overcome boredom and preach messages that inspire, encourage, and inform people about God's Word. Here are just a few:

☐ Grabbing the attention of everyone in the room in the first two minutes gives them a reason to listen to the remainder of your sermon. If you don't, they will check out and count the minutes until your sermon is over.

☑ Relevancy is vital—speak on topics they want to hear and learn about.

☑ Keep your message short. A twenty-five-minute to thirty-five-minute sermon is ideal. Over thirty-five minutes, and you'll start losing people. If you have more to say, make it bonus content. Record what else you wanted to tell them and put it on your website. Or, make it a two-part series and continue the message the following weekend.

☑ Use various tools to get your message across — videos, interviews, quotes, movie clips, lists of funny things you found online, and so forth. Be constantly looking for something you can use as illustrations during your sermons.

☑ Practice your message out loud before Sunday morning, and if possible, get feedback. It is best to do a trial run before Sunday morning with some people and get their feedback. This could be done in a pre-service meeting with your key volunteers, and you could build in a few extra "advanced theology" components to feed your high-level leaders. Also, seek feedback after every sermon you preach.

☑ Watch your previous week's sermon and critique yourself. Did you bore yourself? Did you say anything that a first-time visitor wouldn't understand? Did you go too long? Watch other churches' sermons and see what you liked about theirs and what you didn't like.

☑ Consider getting a coach. There are many professional speaking courses and coaches to help you hone your skills. In the **Church Goals** program, we have several modules on teaching and preaching. Coaching is also a key component of our program. Spend a little time each month dedicated to becoming a better communicator.

There's one other reason to improve your teaching and preaching continually...times change, and so does how we communicate. Go back just two years and listen to how we communicated and used words and phrases. Every year, we invent new words and phrases. Use new words and phrases, and you'll be considered relevant. Use words and phrases that are two years old, and you will be regarded as irrelevant. When many communicators become comfortable using what they think is a new phrase, it's already outdated and will make the communicator look silly. Silly is second to boring in undesirable traits of a communicator.

If you don't feel like you have the time to hone your speaking skills, consider what percentage of your week you should spend on your sermon and sermon prep. How important are Sunday mornings to the success of your church? We believe the most important thing we do as a church is to have fifty-two great weekends. If you followed everyone on our staff and our volunteers each week, you would see this reflected in how they spend their time and budgets to achieve a great weekend experience. I guarantee it will take over 50% of your time to get there. That means if you work a forty-hour week, you should plan on spending a little over twenty hours on your weekend service, of which your sermon is the main event.

## YOU MIGHT WANT TO CONSIDER...

- ☑ Do something monthly to keep your communication skills sharp and cutting edge.
- ☐ Recruit a coach to help you hone your speaking skills.
- ☐ Seek feedback after each time you preach.

☑ Evaluate how much time you spend preparing your
weekly sermon. 50%?

☑ The **Church Goals** program accomplishes each of
the  above. We have modules that will teach you how
to become a better speaker.

## #4—WILL YOU NEED TO BECOME A BETTER LEADER?

What do you believe are the two most important things you do as a leader? We think it's to encourage and support your team. (Side note: That won't happen unless you remain encouraged and are supported too.) People you lead want to be encouraged and supported—encouraged about all aspects of their life and supported in the areas they need to improve. Your job is to lead the people in your church so that when visitors do come, they'll be able to support and encourage them. Part of your leadership will come from encouragement and support through your Sunday morning sermons. The other part is through the one-on-one pastoring of your team. Our goal is to help you lead better in both areas.

I'm always surprised by how many pastors don't feel encouraged and, by extension, are not encouraging to everyone around them. There are two reasons for this. One, many pastors were not encouraged growing up and now don't know how to encourage others. They didn't have encouragement modeled to them. Two, many pastors don't have someone to encourage them and don't know where to find encouragement. Pastors become discouraged because of the pressures of the world and their job. It's hard to encourage others when you are discouraged. Nearly every pastor who goes through the **Church Goals** program becomes encouraged and is equipped and trained to remain encouraged.

Like preaching and teaching, we encourage you to become a lifelong learner when it comes to leadership. A leadership assessment is one of the first things we do in the **Church Goals** program. We want to help you determine your strengths and the areas you need to work on. It's the same thing any coach would do with their team. What are the player's strengths, and where do they need coaching to improve?

Work on the areas that need improvement and become a better leader. Here's the payoff…become a better leader, and you will attract better volunteers who will help you grow your church. Learn how to bring out the best in your team, and they will perform at a higher level. Teach them how to become better leaders, and they will build teams that will help grow your church. Disciple them and show them how they can disciple others.

# YOU MIGHT WANT TO CONSIDER...

☐ Calendar time each month to focus on your leadership skills.

☐ Assess where you need to improve and spend that time each month working on the next area you want to improve.

☐ Learn what encourages you and deploy it daily to remain encouraged and encourage others.

☐ Attend a leadership conference once a year.

# QUESTION
# #3

# DO YOU KNOW HOW TO GROW?

### (GROW)

# 9

# DO PEOPLE KNOW YOU EXIST?

You may think it's obvious that everyone knows your building is a church. That said, we've learned that people can be oblivious to their surroundings. You may think it's obvious that everyone knows they are welcome at your church; however, most people view churches as private clubs where membership is required. Things like denominations may be foreign to them, and they wouldn't know a genuine Christian church from a counterfeit. It's up to you to inform them.

A solid communication plan will let your community know your church is for them. The plan needs to make sure they know you exist, that you want them to come, and that you aren't a private club. They need to know they are welcome and that you have something they are looking for. It should also involve everyone inside your church embracing a culture that invites outsiders into your church.

The bottom line is that most people in your community don't know you exist and don't think they can just walk in. But with some minor tweaks and changes in your church's strategy, you can turn those mindsets around.

## KEY QUESTIONS FOR THIS CHAPTER

1. Do people know you exist?
2. Are you open to "everyone else"?
3. Do you have an inviting culture?
4. Are you active in your community?
5. How is your online presence?

## #1—DO PEOPLE KNOW YOU EXIST?

Many people in your community may drive by your church daily and still not know you exist. One of our campuses is 125,000 square feet (a huge building) on top of a hill on a major street. Every Christmas, we do a light show in the parking lot. We've had people attend the light show and tell us, "I've driven by this building for over ten years and didn't realize it was a church." Really? You didn't see the huge sign on the street with our church's name? You didn't see the twenty-foot cross on top of the building? It taught us that people need something to get their attention and make them see who you are.

Start looking at your church through the lens of an outsider. Is there anything about your church that would convey that you are open on days in addition to Sunday mornings? If you have signs outside your church on Sunday morning, would the unchurched view those signs as directions for church members, or would they apply to them as well?

Many churches put the word "Welcome" on their marquee, but would everyone outside the church think it pertains to them or just to your members? Often churches will put portable signs on the street with the name of their church and an arrow and think the unchurched will see that sign and stop in. While it's true that signs will help those who are looking for your church find it, it's unlikely to think that someone who is driving around on Sunday morning at just the right time and sees your sign will instantly decide to attend a service. Their decision to attend begins way before that.

The signage outside your church should do one of two things: one, draw them to an event at your church other than Sunday morning services (unless you are holding an event in conjunction with the Sunday morning service, like a car show, carnival for the family, or a holiday-related event), and two, show them how to learn more information about your church online. Any signs about an event you are hosting should also point them to your website for more information.

## YOU MAY WANT TO CONSIDER...

- ☐ Use banners and yard signs outside your church to advertise an event at the church.
- ☐ Show your website URL on signs so people can get more information.

### #2—ARE YOU OPEN TO "EVERYONE ELSE"?

Once you get their attention, you must overcome the "private club" and membership hurdles. Most people believe you have to "belong" to that church or denomination to attend. As they drive by, they either consciously or subconsciously think your building is for the "members" of your church. Since they are not members, they may not feel comfortable just showing up.

Yes, we face the challenges of getting people to realize our church exists and to come to check it out. Still, perhaps the greatest challenge is conveying that we are not the Mormon church, Jehovah's Witness church, Christian Science church, or any other counterfeit Christian church...the unchurched person wouldn't know the counterfeit from the genuine. It's up to you to educate them.

The best place to set yourself apart from the private clubs and the counterfeits is your website and social media. We discussed that in chapter 6. Most people will visit your website and look at social media if they become intrigued enough to learn more about your church or consider visiting. This is where they will find your vision, values, and beliefs to give them an informed decision.

## YOU MAY WANT TO CONSIDER...

☐ Update your website and social media and make them "visitor friendly." (This is the first place someone will look who is thinking about visiting your church.)

☐ Will they know the genuine from the counterfeit?

☐ Will they feel welcome at your church?

## #3—DO YOU HAVE AN INVITING CULTURE?

While most congregations would say their church is very inviting, they really aren't inviting people to their church. Statistically, very few people will actually invite someone to church, even if they say they would be open to it. Forget the statistics. Are people in your church bringing their friends and neighbors each week? Is everyone in your church welcoming and friendly to visitors? Do they know to look for them and make them feel welcome?

Remember what we learned in chapter 4 that many people in your church (and possibly even you) don't really want the church to grow. They like the community that's been built and think new people will mess it up. This mentality can be changed. The Core Group meeting is the first step in changing the culture of your church to one that is inviting. The second is to create opportunities for them to invite people to classes, events, small groups, and ministries with a high "yes" response rate. You'll hear more about these possibilities later.

Growth will come when the church's inviting culture equals its welcoming culture. The two go hand-in-hand.

## #4—ARE YOU ACTIVE IN YOUR COMMUNITY?

Are you being the church in your community? Aren't we called to love our neighbor as ourselves? Are we seeking to pursue, please, and meet the needs of others (i.e., demonstrating love)? One of the easiest ways for people to know your church is by you becoming active in their community. We can demonstrate our love for others by helping those in need and interacting with them. Through that process, people will learn about your church and be attracted to it. They will know they are welcome at your church because they will see the people who go there care about them.

There are two ways we recommend becoming active in your community. One is to become active in the events in your community, and the other is through community outreach projects. You will learn more about community outreach projects in chapter 12.

Have you considered the events in neighboring areas and thought about how your church could get involved? Does your community hold any of these events you could get involved with:

| | | |
|---|---|---|
| music festivals | carnivals | picnic days |
| car shows | sporting events | air shows |
| parades | home shows | hobby events |
| seasonal festivals | holiday events | clean-up days |

What if your church had a well-marked booth at each event that did something as simple as providing cold water, popcorn, hot dogs, or any other snack? Your items don't have to be free, but you could bring awareness if you offered something for free as a community service provided by your church.

Call the promoter or sponsor of the event and tell them your church would like to help in any way needed for their event. It could be just providing manpower to help direct traffic or pick up trash. No matter what it is, try to have t-shirts or something that lets people know the church is involved and helping.

It's very easy to get people in your church to "be the church" and go out into the community after the Core Group meeting when your congregants have made it an initiative to become part of the community to reach people for God's Kingdom. The best part is that you won't have to organize your church's involvement personally. God will raise leaders at the Core Group meeting, and you will have people sign up who will want to help.

## YOU MAY WANT TO CONSIDER...

- ☐ Hold your Core Group meeting to determine how you want to get involved in your community.
- ☐ Determine which community events you can easily have a presence at.
- ☐ Be of service somewhere in your community:
  - schools
  - homeless shelters and soup kitchens
  - food banks

## #5—HOW IS YOUR ONLINE PRESENCE?

Pre-Covid, just a handful of churches were known for their television presence. When Covid hit, every church was forced to become an online church. Overnight, people had hundreds of thousands of options to watch church on television or on their computer. People soon realized it was nice to wake up on Sunday morning, stay in their pajamas, make a cup of coffee, and watch church from the comfort of their living room.

Recognizing that people are consumers and want quality, churches soon found out they had to do more than put a mobile phone on a tripod and talk. Congregation members felt some allegiance to their own church but also started surfing the internet for other online churches to see what they offered. Churches with high-quality production began to increase their online viewership dramatically and from all over the world.

At Bayside Church (my home base), we averaged about 20,000 people in seats pre-Covid. We had three days to convert to an online church and thought we would drop to almost nothing. We guessed that 4,000 people would watch our first online church service. We were shocked when over 70,000 people tuned in. And just to qualify those numbers, we only counted unique IP addresses and those who stayed on for at least twenty-five minutes. That number grew to over 200,000 at our online peak. It then dropped to only a handful, but our in-person attendance didn't go back to pre-Covid averages. Where did the people go? Were they not attending church online or in person? While many people were anxious to go back to in-person services, many still liked "pajama church." It's not uncommon now for people to split their time between going in person and watching from home.

Churches dedicated to producing a quality online experience continue to see high online viewership. "Pajama Church" was established and still remains a viable option for many people. So, anyone thinking about visiting a church will do their homework and watch your online services before they attend in person. You'll see in chapter 10 that we can get thousands of people visiting your website every month. They are considering "Church" as a solution to what they are looking for. But when only a handful of those people visit your church, you must conclude they aren't intrigued enough by your website, social media, and online recorded services to want to attend in person.

There are two truths we must conclude from all of this:

1. Churches must improve their online presence (website, social media, and archived messages).
2. Church attendance (at your church) is a hybrid of in-person attendees and online attendees.

To have an effective online presence, you'll first need to address all the questions and comments in chapter 6 about your website being visitor friendly. Looking over those questions, you may already be overwhelmed trying to figure out how to make all those changes to your website. You may not have the bandwidth or the volunteers to make those changes. Luckily, there are several companies whose sole purpose is to help churches create websites that are designed properly, provide a look and feel that consumers expect, and are visitor friendly. Just Google "church website design," and you'll find plenty of companies willing to help.

If you are on a tight budget but have a design sense for what you want your website to look like and know how to design it (so the search engines find what they are looking for), you may want to consider just hiring out to have the coding of the website done by someone else. Several websites provide a platform where people will bid for the opportunity to work on your site, by the hour or project, from all over the world. You can find very skilled coders who have designed and published hundreds of websites and will work for very little. Most of them have designed and coded enough sites to give you examples and ideas to help you create a good site.

Other full-service, Christian-focused website developers and marketing firms understand what people are searching for and how sites should be designed that can provide turnkey solutions. Having worked with hundreds of churches around the world, we at Church Goals have learned that most churches do not have the expertise and manpower, even with volunteers, to put in place a website that works well (is engaging, accomplishes what people are looking for, and, most importantly, converts website clicks into either online or in-person attendees). For this reason, we continue to build a database of marketing companies, web resource companies, and social media experts who can help churches improve their website and social media presence and experience. These resources continue to grow and are available to everyone joining the **Church Goals** program.

Regarding your online church and streaming services, understand that most people will watch a previously recorded sermon or service before they attend in person. You already know from previous chapters that most people have a preconceived notion that when they attend church, they will be bored, they may not understand what's being said, and they may be asked to do things they aren't comfortable doing. You can overcome those hurdles with your online messages.

## PRODUCTION TIPS

Do you just put a camera somewhere in the room and press "record," and then an hour or two later press "stop" and load that onto the internet? Have you gone back and watched your online archived services or messages? Are they interesting and entertaining enough to cause the viewer to want to come to experience your church in person? With just a little effort and direction, you can substantially improve the quality of your online experience, increasing online viewership and in-person attendance. We have recommendations for improving your archived online messages, as well as your live-streaming experiences.

## FOR BETTER ARCHIVED ONLINE MESSAGES...

☑ Edit the recording and only upload the sermon (don't upload the entire service).

☐ Keep your sermons in the sweet spot of twenty-five to thirty-five minutes (you may lose people if your messages are longer).

☐ Record a short intro to the message (less than a minute).

☐ Record an outro that thanks viewers for watching and gives them next steps to take.

☐ Give viewers a way to interact with your church:

- An email address to send prayer requests or questions
- A way to speak to someone in your church
- A way to get involved with or attend an upcoming event or service
- Consider a number they can text to interact with someone immediately
- You may want to consider implementing a chat stream on your website. This has become a very inexpensive and easy tool to implement.

## FOR BETTER LIVE-STREAMING EXPERIENCES...

☐ Use more than one camera.

☐ Have good lighting and sound (use an external microphone, not the internal one on your phone or camera).

☐ An online host to welcome everyone at the beginning of the service and to monitor the chat stream during the service.

☐ A professional production company (for a few hundred dollars, you can get companies that provide cameras and remotely produce your services).

Church is changing; a new normal is being created. We will not experience what was "normal" pre-Covid again. If people went to church once every three weeks before Covid, now they are going once every four to six weeks (in person). People may still consider themselves members or part of your church but also visit other churches online. Pajama church has become real and may be here for a while. There are thousands of choices for online churches to watch because nearly every church created an online presence of some sort when churches were forced to close to in-person visits. Because we live in a consumer-driven society, people have become consumers of churches and now have hundreds of churches to choose from. There are two considerations you should make going forward:

1. For those who already go to church but might pop into your online service on a Sunday to "check it out," make sure it is well done. Follow the tips from this chapter. If you currently have one "in-person" service, know you actually have two services—your online service and your in-person service. Be present with a host in your online service and make everyone feel like they are attending your church in person.

2. For those who are not in church create an online experience and archived recordings that would be attractive to anyone considering attending. Everything they see must convey fun; everyone is welcome, you have what they are looking for, and they will enjoy their online visit as much as their in-person visit.

Anyone considering a visit will do their homework and watch as much as they can find about your church online before they make an in-person visit.

# 10

# WHAT WILL IT TAKE TO GROW?

There are a few things your church can do to bring a steady stream of unchurched people to your church...every month. These things are not hard, and they cost little to no money. We are confident that God has already placed people in your church who will volunteer to help you do these things; you just need to activate and deploy them, which can happen at your Core Group meetings.

All of the concepts in this book are meant to be deployed over a year. In most cases, you only need to spend about an hour a week guiding and directing others (volunteers or staff) who are working on components of the program. This chapter introduces more of those components.

## KEY QUESTIONS FOR THIS CHAPTER

1. Where does growth come from?
2. Is your church findable?
3. Where are people looking?
4. What are they looking for?
5. How can your website help you grow?

6. Have you thought about the business community?

7. How can social media help you grow?

8. Are vocational ministries welcome at your church?

## #1—WHERE DOES GROWTH COME FROM?

Recognizing where church growth comes from can help you focus your strategies on the areas of greatest opportunity. Jason Hamrock with Missional Marketing says that people find their way to church in one of three ways. You can see this depicted in the illustration below.

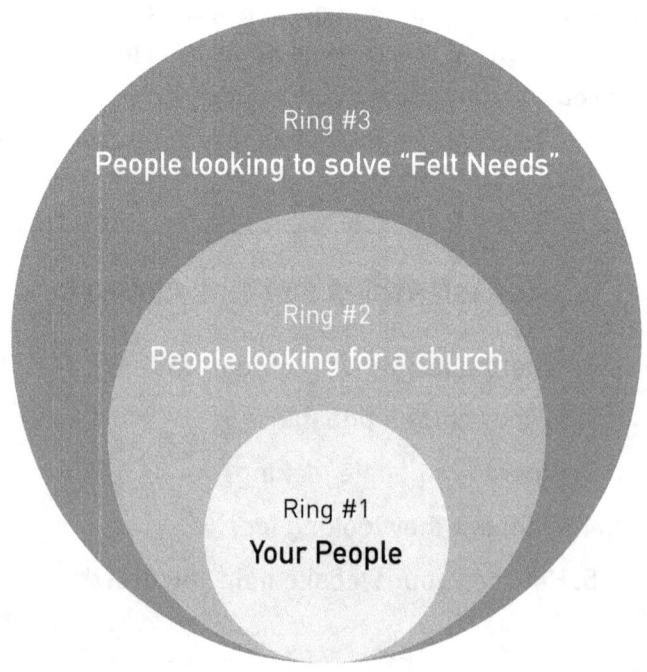

The first ring accounts for the least amount of growth—visitors invited by someone inside your church. Count how many people are in your church. If they all invited one or two people each year, your church would at least double in size. But as we've found, most people in your church are not inviting others, or your church would have constant and steady growth, right?

The second ring represents a much larger opportunity for growth—people in your community who are actively looking for a church. Something happens in their lives that makes them conclude that they should go to church. This might include parents who recently had a baby or have young children and feel responsible for raising their children responsibly. They often conclude they should take them to church. Married couples struggling in their marriage conclude that the church or seeing a pastor might bring a solution. Parents with a spirited teenager conclude that a youth group at the local church might help, among others. In Ring 2, people conclude on their own that the church might provide a solution to what they are going through, and they begin a search for a local church they might attend. Based on search engine analytics, hundreds of people in your community are searching for a church.

The third and largest ring, Ring 3, is for people searching to solve a "felt need" in their life but don't necessarily know the church can provide a solution. Every day, thousands of people in your community are searching for a solution to their "felt need." (We covered felt needs extensively in chapter 7, but it is relevant here again when considering what people search for.) Now that we know this, we need to ensure your church is a solution to their search.

## #2—IS YOUR CHURCH FINDABLE?

If someone has never been to a church and doesn't know how to find one, they might ask a friend where they go or search "church near me" on the internet. If they searched "church near me," where does your specific church show up in their search?

We tried this. We went to the sidewalk in front of our church and typed "church near me" into a phone. Our church showed up on page nine. According to Forbes, less than 6% of people look beyond the first page.[2] That meant we had a very slim chance of anyone finding our church. We showed up on page nine because we hadn't told Google we existed.

Every search engine's primary goal is to match what the searcher is looking for with what they are actually looking for. If the person searching is looking for a church, the search engine wants to show churches in their response. But search engines don't magically know you exist unless you tell them. If you provide the search engine information about your church, you might be listed first when someone is looking for a church that matches your attributes.

The process of informing the search engine is very simple. Go to Google My Business **(https://www.google.com/business/)** and register your church. The service is free and works. We repeated our test. We went out to the sidewalk in front of our church and put in "church near me," and guess what? We were number one on the first page. We were shocked by how many new visitors we had after registering with Google My Business.

---

[2] https://www.forbes.com/sites/forbesagencycouncil/2017/10/30/the-value-of-search-results-rankings/?sh=477e882f44d3ings/?sh=477e882f44d3

Most search engines offer the same service of allowing you to register your church with their search engine for free. Some, like Bing and Yahoo, will enable you to import your Google My Business profile with a few clicks. All of this only takes a few minutes, and you only have to do it once, but the exposure and chances of someone finding your church improve greatly.

In addition to being found online, you'll want to make sure people can find your church while driving to it. We talked about this in chapter 9, but why not make the search a little more festive? We like signs and banners with balloons on the streets approaching the church. Keep in mind that in most cities, they usually must be put up right before and taken down after the service because of sign ordinances. They also will get dirty and start looking bedraggled if left out. These signs are meant to direct people looking for your church, not be advertisements hoping to catch the attention of someone driving by on the off chance they are looking for a church.

## YOU MIGHT WANT TO CONSIDER...

☐ Register your church with search engines like Google My Business.
☐ Place directional signs with balloons on the streets that lead to your church.

### #3—WHERE ARE PEOPLE LOOKING?

It's obvious that people search the internet and social media when looking for anything these days. When they do, will they find your church?

People search for specifics when it comes to churches. It may be that they are looking for a church that has something for their children. They may look for a church that gets good reviews. They might search for a church that meets at a specific time, in a certain part of town, or near where they live. They might be searching for a church based on word of mouth. They may not even be searching for a church, but they find a solution to a problem at a church. So, will they find yours?

You can substantially increase the likelihood that the people searching for a church will find your church if you understand what people are looking for. You need to have those things listed on your website and social media sites. Terms such as *search engine optimization, website optimization,* and *reputation management* are important terms to understand and implement so you can draw people to your church. Pay just a little attention to these three terms, which will help your growth. If you don't have anyone in your church who can help optimize your website, you may want to get help from companies who specialize in it. They can help you improve your find-ability on the internet and social media. Registering with search engines is an example of helping optimization, as discussed above.

If you are overwhelmed by the layer upon layer of things we are bringing up, we understand—it's a lot. We recommend just taking one step at a time. You won't be able to do it all at once, so consider setting aside just one hour a week to work on growing your church. The **Church Goals** program provides resources and a strategic, methodical process to address every question in this book over a year. We'll take it step by step and team you up with a Facilitator who will help you along the way. Working just one hour a week, you will get through it, and your church will grow.

# YOU MIGHT WANT TO CONSIDER...

☐ Optimize your website and social media so people will find what they are looking for. (We will show you what they are looking for in the next section and in greater detail in chapter 11.)

☐ Spend just one hour a week working on your church's growth.

## #4—WHAT ARE THEY LOOKING FOR?

It's all about felt needs. You may recall the list below from chapter 7:

---
### THE TOP TEN FELT NEEDS
---

1. A relationship problem (marriage, divorce, separation, estrangement)

2. Looking to get into a relationship (they are single)

3. An issue with their children or teenagers

4. A financial issue

5. An addiction issue (drugs, alcohol, pornography)

6. A problem at work

7. A health problem

8. They are grieving (recently lost someone).

9. They have a special interest (hobby, sport, or activity) and are looking for that community.

10. They are looking for encouragement and hope (they are fearful, depressed, and discouraged).

The list may change based on what's happening economically, politically, religiously, the time of year, etc. But you can always find what is on people's minds at any given time by looking at what's trending on the search engines. Most search engines provide substantial data on what people are searching for. What if you periodically (like every six to twelve months) looked at what people are concerned about in society, as evidenced by the top ten searches on the most popular search engines, and then made sure your church, website, and social media offered solutions? (You'll see what the solutions can look like in chapter 12.)

Doesn't Jesus Christ provide the solution to every one of the needs listed and any need that could enter the list?

Thousands of people in your community are searching for solutions to these ten felt needs. How can we know? When the **Church Goals** program helps churches prepare for visitors, one of the areas we focus on is their website. We show them how to modify their website to address a solution for their felt needs clearly. The graph below shows actual website analytics of a small church (about 100 people) in the program. Before they deployed the **Church Goals** program, they averaged under 500 new visitors to their website each month (even that's a big number, which tells us people are searching for churches). We then showed them adjustments to their website and how to put their church in a position to be the first or second solution that pops up when someone searches for one of the felt needs. Once the modifications were made, over 3,000 new visitors were hitting their website each month. If several thousand people are hitting your website each month, don't you think some of them might watch your service online or make a visit to your church? This emphasizes the need to make sure your website has what people are looking for and that your church is visitor friendly.

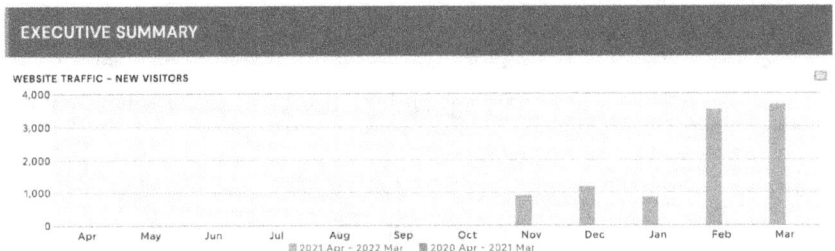

# YOU MIGHT WANT TO CONSIDER...

☐ Offer something on your website and social media sites that indicates you have solutions, like a small group or ministry, for each of the ten felt needs people are trying to solve.

☐ Make sure your website and social media pages present well to first-time visitors, leading them to watch online and then visit in person.

## #5—HOW CAN YOUR WEBSITE HELP YOU GROW?

You need to know several things about how to get your website working for you—keywords, landing pages, and search engine ads. Let's take a look at keywords first.

### KEYWORDS

If someone is searching for a solution to their relationship problem, they might type into their search engine, "how do I fix my marriage" or "my relationship is falling apart." These are called keywords, which are words or phrases users type into the search bar to find information for what they are looking for. In the case of marriage and relationships, keywords might be:

*relationships, fixing marriages, broken relationships, marriage help, marriages falling apart, restoring relationships, restoring marriages*

The search engine will then scan its database to see if there is a website that uses those exact same words, followed by a few other tests to determine if the website is a good fit. It then ranks its findings and delivers those options to the searcher.

## LANDING PAGES

A landing page is a stand-alone webpage that a user "lands" on when they click an ad or a link. The search engines are continually scanning sites and storing data about your site, looking at your headers, sub-headers, descriptions, photos, and links to understand what your site offers.

To make sure your church website is included in the findings, you could have a webpage/landing page on your church's site dedicated to relationships laid out something like this:

**WONDERING HOW TO FIX YOUR MARRIAGE?**
Is your relationship falling apart?

If you've ever asked, "how do I fix my marriage" or "what do I do if my relationship is falling apart," we have something that could help. Come to our six-week class called "Putting the Spark Back in Your Marriage."

This six-week class meets once a week on Wednesday evenings for about an hour and has helped restore the most broken relationships. Before you throw in the towel, give this class a try. We've helped hundreds of couples on the brink of divorce save their marriage.

Click here for more information and to sign up.

In this example, the header and sub-header have some of the keywords used in a search about relationships and marriage. The description uses those keywords, too. Additionally, the photo looks like someone in a relationship. The search engine would rank this landing page near the top of the search list because many of the words matched exactly what the person was searching for. If the search engine recognizes you are a church (through Google My Business), you could further enhance your search position since churches are known for providing counseling services and pastoral advice for marriage. It would confirm you are in the business of "relationships" and improve the ranking and your position on the page.

Your website traffic will increase if you have a similar-looking landing page for each of the felt needs people are searching for. This is why the graph above showed a jump in first-time visitors.

There is likely someone already in your church who would love to volunteer their time to help keep your website up-to-date relating to what people are searching for. You just have to activate and deploy them. If you need help doing that, you guessed it... the **Church Goals** program can help.

## SEARCH ENGINE ADS

There's one other way that will substantially improve your ranking on the page. You can advertise on the search engine using the felt needs as your focus in the advertisement. You can likely do this for free. Google offers grants to nonprofits. Nearly all churches are nonprofits, meaning free advertising every month. You can run an ad and list the keywords you want to be associated with the ad that then points to the part of your website associated with the felt need. For example, you could run an ad using the keywords mentioned on page 146. The ad could then point directly to the appropriate landing page of your website about fixing your marriage.

When someone searches for anything using Google, the search engine first looks to see if anyone has paid for an advertisement related to the search. If yes, it will show that listing first. In the example below, people often search for "comfort" as a felt need. They could type in "places providing comfort in (my town)"; we used Bakersfield, CA, in this example. You will see that the first two solutions provided (out of 269,000 results) are churches. Both churches ran an ad (for free because they utilized Google's free advertising for nonprofits) that used the keyword "comfort." You can see this was a paid ad because the first line starts with the word Ad.

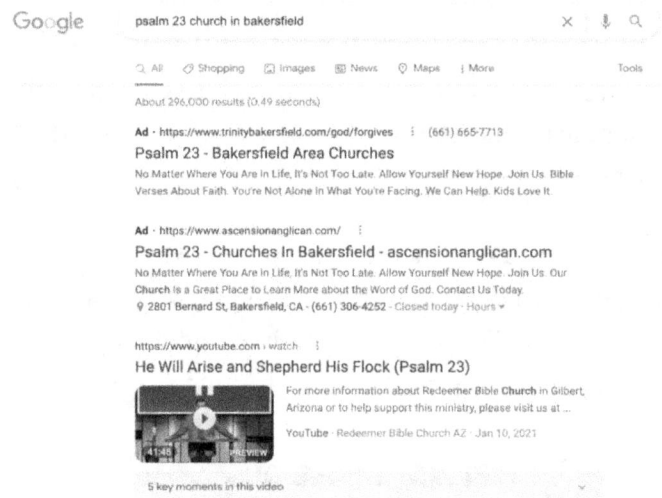

Qualifying for Google's free advertising is fairly simple, and most churches qualify. Not quite so easy is placing all the ads and managing them. This is important because Google has design and performance guidelines that must be met. There are companies that manage Google advertising and compliance for not a lot of money (a fraction of what the ads would normally cost). The **Church Goals** program maintains a list of companies that will help you get free advertising and manage all of it. Visit churchgoals. org for a list of resources to help manage search engine advertising.

# YOU MIGHT WANT TO CONSIDER...

☐ Placing "landing pages" on your website for each of the ten felt needs.

☐ Applying for free advertising with Google.

☐ As part of the **Church Goals** program, we will apply for the grant for you and show you the best way to have it managed (by others).

## #6—HAVE YOU THOUGHT ABOUT THE BUSINESS COMMUNITY?

Few churches have anything to offer the work world. In the mid-1990s, I owned a business that converted paper to electronic files. We had over 100 employees, most of whom were low-wage earners. When you pay people close to minimum wage, turnover is very high. I had a hard time attracting and keeping employees and needed to know what changes I could make. Study after study said the top five things people want in the workplace are:

1. Enjoy the people they work with (good employee relations)
2. Fulfill the contract (produce something of value for the company in exchange for their wage)
3. Rules or core values (people want to work for companies with a positive mission and vision and who are honest and ethical)
4. Recognition for the job they've done (it's as simple as thanking them for their work)
5. Money (unless they don't get 1–3 above, then money moves to number one)

As I studied how to build these into my company, I learned that the top three things on the list were things God wants from us. The first two are based on loving people, the second most important thing to God (Matthew 22:39), and the third relates to the most important thing to God, loving Him with all our heart, mind, soul, and strength (Matthew 22:37). I learned that if I set the right goals, found the right people to accomplish those goals, and then incorporated daily processes to ensure they would accomplish all five things on the list, they and the company would thrive. The **Business Goals** program was born, followed by the **Church Goals** program, when we saw the same principles applied to churches.

At the church where I worked, we held a **Business Goals** class for business owners, business leaders, and literally anyone who had a job. In the very first session, I would announce two requirements for being part of the class. First, when their business became more successful because they were implementing biblical principles into their workplace, they had to give credit where credit was due—to God. They could do that by tithing. I made it clear that they weren't to just give to the church but to tithe a full 10%. Second, they had to fill their seat. I told them if they found the class valuable, tell someone else who could fill their seat once they were done with the class.

The outcomes of these two requirements were amazing. About three to six months after a class ended, I was always surprised to find that giving would go up by $25,000 to $50,000 when annualized. I didn't make a big deal about it, but I called several of the people and asked if they hadn't been tithing before the class and then started after the class. Every person I spoke to said they had always tithed, but because their business was doing so much better, they were making more and tithing more. This has remained consistent with every class.

We never expected the second outcome from the classes. Attendees were filling their seats with people who had never been to church. The class is mostly secular in nature and very attractive to the unchurched, so it became common for half of every class to fill with people from outside the church. As each session progressed, those people became friends with others in the class, and many began attending our church. It became an unintended outreach.

Part of the growth strategy for churches in the **Church Goals** program is to launch the **Business Goals** ministry in month three (after they go through some necessary steps to prepare for visitors). Launching the **Business Goals** ministry offers a place to serve in the church for business professionals and for people who know a lot about business and management. In nearly every class, someone from the church tells us, "This is a great ministry; how can I get involved in it?" or "Finally, the church has a ministry I can relate to and want to participate in." We encourage anyone who wants to become involved in the ministry to become a Facilitator for the next class. Any class graduate can become a Facilitator after a simple training program. Business leaders and professionals are now serving where they can thrive and are excited about it.

The **Business Goals** ministry also becomes the "farm team" or incubator for your leadership team, Elder board, or church governance. This is another unexpected outcome. The **Business Goals** class attracts business leaders, business owners, and people who want to lead. You most likely have business people who have been in your church for years and are spiritually advanced whom God has put in your church to serve. You just need to activate and deploy them. The **Business Goals** class can become the boot camp that preps them for a leadership role in your church.

The **Business Goals** classes are only six weeks long and meet for about an hour each week. There are about ten to twelve people in each class with one Facilitator. The people in the classes usually become friends and often want to continue meeting as a group after the class ends. Several small groups (life groups) have formed out of **Business Goals** classes. Isn't this what we want? Shouldn't you start a ministry for business owners, business leaders, and everyone who works?

## YOU MIGHT WANT TO CONSIDER...

☑ Launch a **Business Goals** ministry at your church. Go to businessgoals.org for more information or scan this QR code:

## #7—HOW CAN SOCIAL MEDIA HELP YOU GROW?

As I mentioned earlier, there are over eighty social media sites. When someone is looking for a church or deciding if they want to visit one they've heard about or saw an ad for, they will visit the church's website and social media sites—you can count on it. Your social media sites can help you grow your church...but they must be visitor-friendly and provide the information people want.

Think of your website as an online billboard. Your social media sites are also online billboards, allowing people to make comments. That can either be dangerous or advantageous. People who have a bad experience at your church might leave negative comments on your social media or other sites. Of course, they might leave good comments if they have a good experience. Good or bad, you need to respond. Since many, many people use reviews to decide if they want to try something, you do want people to interact with your social media sites. Still, you want to mitigate any negative or potentially damaging threads. The more interactive you are with social media, the more people will interact. Having a continual stream of new information on your sites will get people interested and engage your sites. You'll get people talking about your church, but you want to make sure it's positive and not negative.

From previous chapters, you know people may have pre-conceived notions that church will be boring, confusing, or a private club. You can use your billboards (website and social media) to counter those notions. You can put photos of people having fun at your last church event or people smiling on Sunday morning. When posting anything on your website or social media, beware of using Christian lingo. Avoid words from the list in chapter 6 and words like fellowship, brother Bob or sister Betty, worship, communion...you get the idea. When posting photos and describing events, make them inclusive versus exclusive. Show that everyone in your community is welcome.

Another way to use social media to grow your church is by promoting your upcoming events, including weekend services. Specialize it to appeal to the person reading the post instead of a generic post to the whole world. You can do this by posting your upcoming event on your social media site. Include some photos from a previous event if you have them, and be specific about who should attend the event. If the event is for kids, say so in the title of the post. For example, you might be holding a fall event around Halloween for families in your community. Your title might be, COME TO FESTIFALL!! FUN FOR THE WHOLE FAMILY, AND YOUR KIDS WILL LOVE IT.

Finally, consider a recommended strategy from CJ Alvarado of Bamboo Creative, who is an expert in church marketing and communications. You post something every day from the content you've created on the weekend—your sermon. You take pieces of your sermon and send them out every day on social media using a deliberate process. For example…

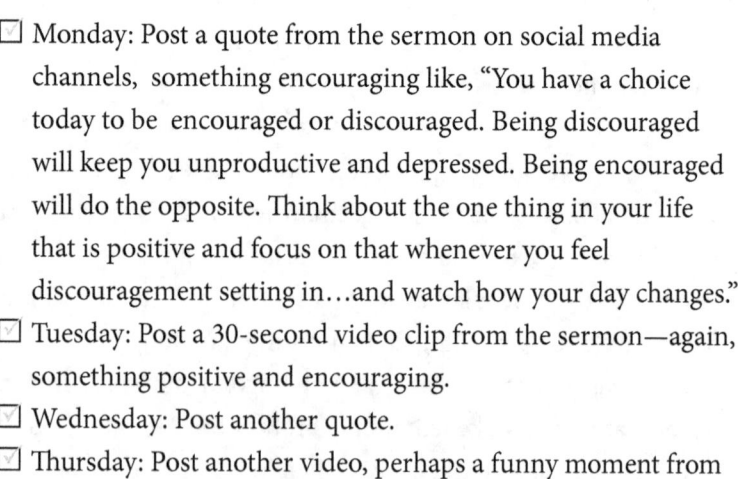

- ☑ Monday: Post a quote from the sermon on social media channels, something encouraging like, "You have a choice today to be encouraged or discouraged. Being discouraged will keep you unproductive and depressed. Being encouraged will do the opposite. Think about the one thing in your life that is positive and focus on that whenever you feel discouragement setting in…and watch how your day changes."
- ☑ Tuesday: Post a 30-second video clip from the sermon—again, something positive and encouraging.
- ☑ Wednesday: Post another quote.
- ☑ Thursday: Post another video, perhaps a funny moment from

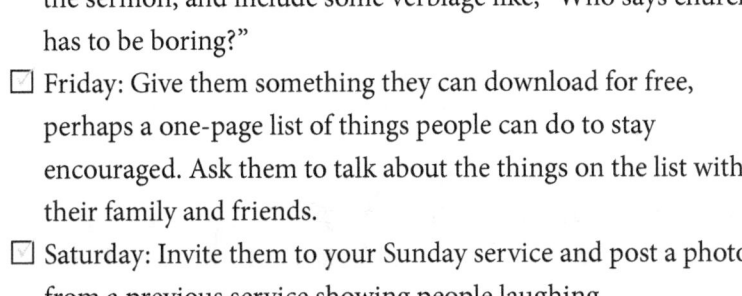

the sermon, and include some verbiage like, "Who says church has to be boring?"

☑ Friday: Give them something they can download for free, perhaps a one-page list of things people can do to stay encouraged. Ask them to talk about the things on the list with their family and friends.

☑ Saturday: Invite them to your Sunday service and post a photo from a previous service showing people laughing.

This might sound like a lot of work, but it can become simple and routine. There are likely youths in your church who live on social media. Get serious about the Youth Ministry Module discussion in chapter 11 and activate two teens in your church to own social media. Maybe it's an internship or a small part-time job. Kids are looking for real-world experience, and you can give it to them. Plus, it will be a big deal to meet with you, their senior pastor, every week to be discipled (that's what you can give them in return).

So you know, there are tools out there that help manage all eighty-plus social media sites. They allow you to monitor social sites so that if anyone posts anything about you or your church, you are alerted and can respond. They also have automatic responses that can be sent if the incoming post doesn't demand a response. For example, someone posts that they had a great time at your church, and the system responds, "Thanks for being part of (your church)." The tools also allow you to post on all sites at once. You can deploy CJ's strategy in just a few minutes each day to all sites. Visit the churchgoals.org website for a list of social media automation resources.

There's one last thing that we've learned that people want most from their church. CJ Alvarado and his team spent a year watching where people interacted—social media, websites, advertisements, etc. They discovered that people want a daily boost from their senior pastor and a deeper connection to them. You can accomplish both with a daily devotion to everyone who wants it.

In 2011, we had the idea of sending out a two-minute daily devotional to anyone who wanted it via text. I asked two close friends, Troy Krutoff and Rob Bagley, who owned Blit—a computer software company. I asked if they could create a software program for free that would make it easy to send out this daily devotional. In short order, they created the software we named Refuel. We told our congregation they could text the word Refuel to 56316 and sign up for the daily devotional. Every morning at 7:00 a.m. (Monday – Friday), we sent a video from our senior pastor. It was something short but encouraging. We started hearing stories of how people felt a connection to the pastor through that devotional. It brightened up their day. It gave them hope to keep moving forward. It was starting their day with a connection to their pastor and God instead of facing the junk the world was pushing at them.

Through word of mouth, our social media channels, our website, and from hearing about Refuel at our conferences, we now have over 20,000 people receiving positive and encouraging news to start their day (you can sign up for it too—just text Refuel to 56316).

Today, many companies offer similar texting options like what Troy and Rob created. You can find a list of companies on the **Church Goals** website (churchgoals.org). I encourage you to put social media to work for your church. It is one more piece of the many little things you can do to be relevant, provide what people are looking for, and help grow your church.

# YOU MIGHT WANT TO CONSIDER...

- ☑ Make social media a part of your church growth plan.
- ☑ Update your social media pages regularly—daily is ideal.
- ☐ Find young people in your church to "own" your social media accounts.
- ☑ Make your social media pages depict anything but boring.
- ☐ Send out daily devotionals (daily is best, but twice or three times a week is good too).

## #8—ARE VOCATIONAL MINISTRIES WELCOME AT YOUR CHURCH?

People are always trying to predict what will cause the next growth spurt in their church or business. One of the predictions is that vocational ministries will lead Church growth over the next twenty years. It's no surprise given that vocational ministries can provide solutions to some of the felt needs that push people to seek out a church.

DivorceCare is a vocational ministry that provides a logical solution for relief from the grief of failed marriages. If someone is struggling at work, **Business Goals** is a vocational ministry that can get them back on track. If someone is having problems with addiction, Celebrate Recovery is a good vocational ministry to introduce them to. For people suffering from losing a loved one, GriefShare provides support and resources to help them move forward. Principles to Live By is another vocational ministry that provides marriage and family resources and support.

Whether this is a prediction about the future growth of the church or not, your church will grow by offering vocational ministry opportunities through your church. How? These ministries have a great track record of attracting unchurched people to their ministry. When people are on your campus attending the ministry event, meeting, and getting to know people from inside the church, who are attending the same event, and seeing and hearing about the good things your church does and has to offer… these unchurched people will likely check out your church, especially if they are invited. But there's a specific process to follow in moving people from attending the vocational ministry to visiting a Sunday morning service. You'll read about that in chapter 12.

## YOU MIGHT WANT TO CONSIDER…

- ☑ Make a list of vocational ministries your church might offer.
- ☑ See how many of those ministries you can launch in the next twelve months.

# ARE YOU WILLING TO EXPAND?

(EXPAND)

# DO YOU HAVE WHAT PEOPLE ARE LOOKING FOR?

If you surveyed everyone in your community based on how they were doing in general, what do you think the results would look like? While many people will complain about something, if you press them to answer the question, all things considered, the results might surprise you. 10% to 15% of your community would likely have some crisis taking place in their lives. Another 10% to 15% would have something exciting taking place. And 70% to 80% of the people would tell you that life is "okay." The point is that most people are just doing life. They are not in a bad season, nor are they in a good season.

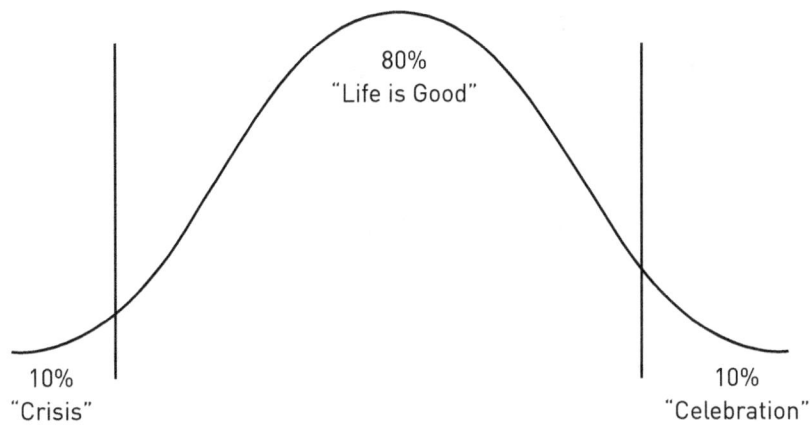

80%
"Life is Good"

10%
"Crisis"

10%
"Celebration"

Regardless of which category people are in, everyone is looking for something that will meet the needs of their current situation. Those in crisis will seek a solution to help them through their crisis. Those celebrating something great will be looking for people to tell about this great thing and celebrate with them. The big group in the middle will be looking for activities that allow them to be in community with others who might enjoy the things they enjoy. The percentages don't matter. What matters is that there are people in all three stages in your community.

Meeting the needs of these three groups requires churches to EXPAND their offerings to reach their community. Does your church have what people are looking for? Suppose your church is part of that community and designed to create community. Shouldn't you be offering events, ministries, and activities that mirror what people in your community want and need? Is your church ready to expand?

## KEY QUESTIONS FOR THIS CHAPTER

1. What are you doing for people looking for a social outlet and community?
2. What are you doing for people looking for a mission or purpose?
3. Are you giving people an excuse to come to church?
4. How can you make your church fun with interesting services?

## #1—WHAT ARE YOU DOING FOR PEOPLE LOOKING FOR A SOCIAL OUTLET AND COMMUNITY?

Not everyone thinking about coming to church is in crisis. There are more healthy people in the world than hurting people, at least in their minds. Your church will see great growth if you become a "home for the healthy" in addition to a "hospital for the hurting." So, what are the healthy looking for? Some are looking for a social outlet and community.

This should come as no surprise as God created us to be in relationship—with Him and with others. He also put in us a desire to be in relationships. Shouldn't we help facilitate and accomplish both at the same time? Isn't that what loving your neighbor is all about?

Many don't think about the church when looking for social outlets and places to meet people. But we can provide an outlet to meet the need to be in relationships with other people, and then while they are cultivating their relationships with people, introduce them to the relationship with God.

Even though some people think churches are boring, ask for money, and are sometimes confusing or judgmental, we know that's not what we are about—that's just the stigma attached to us that sometimes gets exacerbated by us being human and doing church without thinking about first-time visitors. Churches are made up of broken people who make mistakes just like everyone else. But don't we like doing many things the people outside the church like doing, too? So why not bring the two together? You already have a few events that bring people into your church: Christmas, Easter, and perhaps a few random days of the year. That said, other opportunities make sense, too. Could you start ministries to create events/venues that bring people together and could also introduce them to Christ? YES, you can.

Consider Adventure Sports. Adventure Sports is a ministry that Greg Weisman started at Bayside Church over 20 years ago. It began with a small group of people who wanted to go dirt bike riding, and they invited Greg, our Middle School pastor at the time. Before the ride, everyone went around and introduced themselves and said what they did professionally. Greg, of course, said he was a pastor. He also asked if he could pray for everyone's safety before the ride, and nobody objected. Everyone had a great time riding dirt bikes, and aside from the prayer, nothing was ever said about God, Jesus, the Bible, or Church.

At the end of the day, everyone agreed that they would like to get together for another bike ride the following week. They did, and it went very similarly. A few new people came, introductions were made, and Greg prayed for everyone's safety on the ride. At the end of the ride, Greg mentioned that he was thinking about starting a small group during the week and invited everyone there to attend—he made it clear that it didn't matter if they went to church or not. Some came, and a small group of people who liked dirt bikes were now studying God's Word mid-week together. But the group continued to grow and grow and grow. More events were added. Camping trips, fishing trips, skiing trips, and other sporting events.

It became clear from Greg's experience that gathering groups of people based on their hobbies and interests was very easy. Some people decided they liked to watch football on television…they started a group. Some people wanted to take bucket list trips…they started a group. People were in community doing what they liked and invited God into the mix. You can do this, too.

It's an easy ministry to start. You need no money, and very little training, and everyone in the church can either start a group or be a part of a group because everyone has hobbies and interests. Have someone say a prayer before the event, do the event, and invite them to a mid-week Bible study with their new friends. You've now created a social outlet based on the things they like most and then introduced them to God.

Need another example? There was a woman in the church who liked to sew. She invited a few friends to get together one Saturday a month and decided to sew dresses for young girls whose families could never afford new dresses. The group got together, made patterns, and sewed dresses. They named their ministry "Dress a Girl." Eventually, the group decided to buy sewing machines. They ended up getting a substantial discount on the sewing machines, other necessary machines, and supplies because the store liked their ministry. They even got some of the equipment donated. What a great example of the church and community working together for a greater cause!

One ministry started for people who liked to work on cars. Initially, they got together to work on their own vehicles, many of which were show cars, but then it grew into working on cars for the people in their church who needed help but couldn't afford it. A similar ministry started with bicycles that led to collecting bicycles, repairing them, and giving them out at Christmas to kids whose families couldn't afford gifts.

In each of these ministries, the ministry started because people took their hobby and turned it into a ministry. They invited people with similar interests, then weaved a Bible study into it.

Here's the bottom line. We know that everyone needs God in their lives, but sometimes, they don't know it and are reluctant to go to church. That said, God is tugging on their hearts to know Him just like He did with you and me. Give people an easy onramp to church by incorporating it into their hobbies and including their friends. They will come.

If you want more information on Adventure Sports, they provide a host of resources to help you launch this ministry at your church. Here's the link: https://www.baysideadventuresports.com/. The **Church Goals** program also provides extensive details on other ministries your church can launch.

People are looking for a social outlet and a sense of community. Give them the best one they could ever be a part of—the Church.

## YOU MIGHT WANT TO CONSIDER...

- ☑ Recognize that every event you have at your church could be meeting the needs of those looking for a social outlet and community.
- ☑ Have every person in your church turn their hobby or special interest into a ministry.
- ☑ Resources are available to help start special interest and hobby-based ministries or small groups.

### #2—WHAT ARE YOU DOING FOR PEOPLE LOOKING FOR A MISSION OR PURPOSE?

K-Love radio once held a conference for millennials. They invited various millennial leaders from around the country and had them speak on trends, how millennials think, what they like, and what they want to be a part of. One of the key points I came away with was that millennials want to be part of something with a purpose and a mission that feeds the greater good. They want to work for companies with strong core values and produce something good for society. Gen Zers want the same thing. I don't think these desires are unique to millennials and Gen Zers. I think they apply to everyone. Nobody wants to be part of a company that produces something bad for society or cheats and steals to get ahead.

People are looking for the same attributes in the Church. They want a church actively engaged in and doing something good for the community. Is your church doing this? One of the easiest ministries to create is community service ministries, especially those that serve amidst disasters. The church should be known for stepping up in times of great need to provide help. We should be known for our compassion ministries and projects.

I live in Northern California. Several years ago, an arsonist lit a fire in our local mall. The mall had to close for about six months to repair all the damage. We heard hundreds of families would be financially impacted by the loss of jobs due to the closure. We took a second offering to supplement their loss of income and help keep those families from financial ruin. We raised enough money that when everyone returned to work, we still had money left over.

The Tubbs fire destroyed over 5,000 homes and devastated the Santa Rosa community. We have a church campus in Santa Rosa and offered it to Cal Fire, who used it as a base station. We also took a second offering and raised enough money to help Convoy of Hope bring several loads of supplies to those who were displaced.

The following year, the town of Paradise was destroyed by the Camp fire. Over 18,000 structures were lost. The largest church in town was miraculously spared but went from 3,000 attendees on a weekend to just a few hundred. We took the entire church staff through the **Church Goals** program in a one-day intensive, helped them establish a plan for the next year, and encouraged them to be strong. The senior pastor called me six months later, saying they had already met their one-year plan. They had opened a second campus, where most of the displaced families had moved, and were now running services in two communities on Sundays. The church survived and thrived.

One of the results of being a church known for its involvement in our community is attracting people who want to be part of that mission. We have grown because of our expansion into compassion-minded projects.

In addition to responding quickly when disaster strikes, we also plan projects to help our community. We designate a particular weekend as "Serve Day," where we close our doors (that's right—no regular church service) and ask everyone to work on a community service project instead. Throughout the year, our volunteers in charge of Serve Day look for potential activities: schools asking for landscaping or painting, parks that need bark or freshening up, collecting trash around homeless camps, and elderly people whose homes need a once-a-year yard clean-up. Children are undergoing significant health issues, and we brighten up their day by doing a makeover in their bedroom. We set up one-day clinics for health screenings, free dental exams, and simple repairs. The list goes on. Our last Serve Day had over 100 community projects and over 10,000 people participating. We also had nearly 100% of the necessary materials donated by local businesses. We had everything we needed to be "the Church" and impact the community.

Don't think you can pull off something like this? Don't think you can close your church for a weekend because you'll lose the tithe income for that weekend? We prepared for weeks in advance by continually telling our congregation we were all going to work, and they all needed to remember to tithe, so the church doesn't falter financially. We never missed a beat on the finances, and nearly everyone worked on some project. We then held a great celebration on Sunday night of the Serve Day weekend, with reports on the work that had been done and the impact it had on the people in our community.

If you're worried your church is too small to pull something like this off, think about the one or two projects your people can work on during a weekend. Something is way better than nothing. Meet with your mayor or school district and look for the greatest need. As you get the word out about your community service projects, ask people if they want to help. Those 10,000 people were not all from our church. Hundreds were people who got invited to help along the way. Many of them came to our celebration and church the following weekend. People want to be a part of doing something good for their community—they just need an opportunity to do so, which churches can provide.

You can do more than periodic events. Why not do monthly events? Start a community service ministry in your church. God has already put a few people in your congregation to head this ministry. You can serve the homeless one day a month. You can volunteer at the local food bank once a month. If you have an aging congregation, maybe they could help elementary school students learn to read. There is something for everyone. And this ministry costs nothing to start. It just requires the manpower you already have in your church.

When we ask our congregation what they like about our church, they always put our community involvement and desire to serve the community at or near the top of the list. People desire to be part of something with a great mission and purpose. The best part? We get to introduce people to Christ along the way.

The **Church Goals** program has a step-by-step process on initiating and running community service projects and starting a community outreach ministry in your church. Our third quarter (EXPAND) is dedicated to walking you through a step-by-step process of expanding your church's small groups and ministries to meet the needs of those in your community.

## YOU MIGHT WANT TO CONSIDER...

☑ If you don't have a mission statement that conveys you are missional toward your community...create a mission statement that:
- Any unchurched person would be attracted to
- Your community would embrace and get behind
- Everyone (including the unchurched) would understand
- Is short, concise, and compelling
- Everyone remembers and can repeat
- Is measurable and obtainable
- Is evergreen (lasts a long time)

☑ Create a disaster preparedness program so your church can respond to needs quickly.

☑ Prepare your congregation to be mission- and service-minded.

☑ Show compassion in your community by taking a second offering to support those in need when local disasters occur.

☑ Start 2–3 ongoing ministries committed to serving your community.

## #3—ARE YOU GIVING PEOPLE AN EXCUSE TO COME TO CHURCH?

Is your church the "in" place to be on Sunday morning? If yes, way to go. If not, why not? Did you ever feel that Starbucks or the local café is the "in" place to be? Why can't your church become the "in" place to be instead? It can!

People want to go to fun places. They want to be seen and be a part of their community. Why not create a venue that does that? Instead of going to the mall and walking around, why not make your church inviting enough that people want to come there on Sunday morning? And other mornings, too!

You can start by picking an upcoming holiday or special day and making it a party. What is a party? One definition of a party is a social gathering of guests, typically involving eating, drinking, and entertainment. So, invite everyone in your community to your event, provide some food and drinks like coffee and donuts, and make your sermon entertaining… and you have a party. If you plan the event on a Sunday, it can incorporate them coming to church.

Take Father's Day, for example. We decided to hold a car show at our church one Father's Day weekend. First, we went to several other car shows, contacted several car clubs, and invited them to show their cars at our event. We had no problem filling our parking lot. We actually had to have people register to show their cars because we had too many! Then, we went online and learned all we could about what the people with the cars liked about shows they attended. What did they want? Being invited, eating, drinking, and providing some entertainment. In a word, a party. So we created a party! We had donuts and coffee, gave everyone who showed their car a small plaque for attending (less than $5 each), and awarded prizes for the cars everyone liked the most. (A group of our volunteers learned about judging the cars and established categories.) We put signs in front of our church advertising the show a few weeks in advance and posted them on social media and our website. It worked.

That Father's Day, show cars arrived as early as we told them they could (like 6:30 a.m.), and we lined them up in the parking lot. We had our donuts and coffee ready and invited them to attend the church service later that morning. As the community started coming to see the cars, we invited them to attend the church service, too. Not everyone did, but some did. The event became a tradition. Our last car show had over 5,000 people from the community attend. We gave people a reason to come to our church, and they did.

Whether people come to events like the car show simply to engage in a hobby or because they are intrigued by God and need an excuse to learn more, it allows them to connect with the church, and it gives us a chance to talk to them about our church and invite them back.

Here's one more example: a Christmas Lights Drive-Thru. Our senior pastor had visited a church that put up lights in their parking lot at

Christmas and invited their community to drive through the parking lot and see them. It seemed pretty simple, so we tried it. We had a fairly large parking lot, spoke to a few consultants who were experts on drive-thru Christmas displays, and put together a group of volunteers from our church who liked to hang Christmas lights. We were told by the consultants that we had to charge money and that we had to provide ticketing or we would have huge traffic problems. We were committed to providing this event for free (we didn't want the community to think the church was making a profit on Christmas), but we did come up with a ticketing solution in case the consultants were right. We didn't require tickets the first night because we didn't think many people would come. We hadn't advertised it other than doing what we did for the car show...a few signs out front and postings on social media and our website. We were shocked. We had traffic backed up for five miles in every direction. The police and neighbors weren't very happy with us, so the next day, we turned on the ticketing system requiring tickets and solved our traffic problems.

We had over 79,000 people come through our Christmas Lights Drive Thru that first year, which was open for about thirty days between Thanksgiving and New Year's Eve). Once again, our church was the place everyone in the community wanted to visit, and we invited them to come back on Sunday morning. Because we implemented a ticketing system that captured their email address, we could see if anyone had started attending church due to our Christmas Lights Drive Thru. About six months after the light show, we would look at our database to see if anyone had started tithing regularly whose first entry into our database was the Christmas Lights Drive Thru. To our surprise, we grew by about ninety tithing families each year because of the light show.

You're probably thinking how that was a major undertaking, probably cost thousands of dollars (it did), and is completely out of your league. It doesn't have to be that big. We have consulted with many churches that were very small but wanted to do something at Christmas for their community, like a Christmas lights display or drive-thru. You can do something on a smaller scale and still impact your church, the community, and the Kingdom of God.

There are people in your congregation right now that you can activate and deploy to help put on events like these. These are not hard events to pull off. If you don't want to do an event that might get too big, start small. Put a few bounce houses out front and have a free pancake breakfast for the community on some random Sunday. Advertise it for a few weeks before the event, and people will show up. Make the weekend especially fun for the kids in Sunday school, and they will want to come back and drag their parents with them (who, deep down inside, know church is the place they should be on Sunday morning). You can do this. I guarantee it.

## YOU MIGHT WANT TO CONSIDER...

- ☑ Hold a few events at your church each year that draws people from your community to your church (in addition to Christmas and Easter).
- ☑ Turn your events into parties...invite them, feed them, entertain them (yes, your service can be entertaining).

## #4—HOW CAN YOU MAKE YOUR CHURCH FUN WITH INTERESTING SERVICES?

I see nowhere in the Bible that says church can't be fun. God has a sense of humor and created us in His image, so we must have a sense of humor and make church fun, too. So much more goes into making something fun. People will have fun when they connect with others and have a shared experience and when doing the things they like. If your services are fun, interesting, and relevant to their lives, when they are a bit entertained and amused and when you give them something to think about, they will have fun. They will have fun if you can help their kids and other family members to enjoy themselves. All these things can be incorporated into a Sunday service. If people want to have fun as a condition for coming to church, let's make it fun. After all, fun is a solution to being boring.

Here are some recommendations we deploy regularly to make church services fun:

- ☐ Deploy a hospitality team whose purpose is to "make it fun."
- ☐ Build your messages around a theme (current events and the season can be popular)
- ☐ Have volunteers dress according to the theme —make it a party
- ☐ Use funny videos (YouTube has thousands)
- ☐ Teach in all four learning styles as discussed in chapter 6
- ☐ Make free food part of your Sunday services (bagels and donuts are cheap and popular)
- ☐ Make it fun for the kids—make whatever they are interested in available

☑ Give positive and encouraging messages (save the fire and brimstone for later)

☑ Make your messages relevant (see chapter 7)

☑ Have weekends that honor or recognize worthy groups of people (i.e., first responders, teachers, veterans, etc.)

☑ Speak to everyone, not just the Christians in the room

☑ Meet people where they are by designing your sermon and weekend for your community

☑ Include young people—everyone likes hanging out with people younger than them

☑ Determine what people find interesting and include it in your sermon

☑ Create a church that mirrors your community (if your community is diverse, make your church diverse…by age, ethnicity, cultural background, etc.)

If you set the tone for the weekend as one that's going to be fun, it will be fun. If people don't think of you as a fun person, find people in your church who are fun and have them help you. Who would everyone say at your church are the two most fun people to have in the room? Put them in charge of hospitality for weekends. Tell them their goal is to make the weekend festive and enjoyable.

When we were looking to launch a new Sunday night service, the first thing we did was recruit someone whom everyone loved having in the room. She built a small team and created an exciting atmosphere each Sunday night. One week it was s'mores around fire pits; the next, it was blended iced mochas, then a nacho bar. Some evenings were built around the sporting event of the season, like the Super Bowl or World Series, and everyone was encouraged to wear their favorite team's jersey. Sunday evening became our most popular service, with people still receiving a great Bible-based message and a positive impact.

## YOU MIGHT WANT TO CONSIDER...

- ☑ Deploy the recommendations provided into your services.
- ☐ Recruit two volunteers whose single purpose is to make services fun.
- ☑ Remember that these are simple steps — you can do it!

# WILL YOU EXPAND IN THE AREAS NECESSARY TO GROW?

God has given you everything you need to grow and expand your church. He's put people in your midst who are just waiting to be activated and deployed into ministry. He's put you in charge as someone to gather and lead His people. He's placed you in a community longing for a Savior—they just may not know that yet. Perhaps He might have even prompted you to read this book containing the next set of instructions for you to take to grow and expand.

## KEY QUESTIONS FOR THIS CHAPTER

1. Does your church have ministry solutions for some or all of the ten felt needs?

2. How can you connect people to your solutions for their felt needs?

3. How do I activate the troops God gave me?

## #1—DOES YOUR CHURCH HAVE MINISTRY SOLUTIONS FOR SOME OR ALL OF THE TEN FELT NEEDS?

If a first-time visitor came to your church next Sunday and told you they were struggling in their marriage and thought the church might have a solution, what would you do for them? We know Christ is the solution to every problem in their life, but do you have a tangible resource that helps them with their specific issue and directs them to Christ? You might tell the person you could meet with them and tell them that church, in general, will help. But that solution won't produce the same results as being able to direct them to a small group focused on strengthening and healing marriages or a four-week class on building marriages that last.

How can you create a solution for each of the felt needs people are searching for? It's a matter of putting in place a ministry or small group for each of the felt needs. Resources are available to equip volunteers in your church to start and lead these small groups or ministries.

Hopefully, you're beginning to see your role and responsibility changing at your church. In the past, you might have tried to be everything and do everything for each member of your congregation. Your role needs to change to creating disciples who create disciples. What if you focused on finding ten to twelve volunteers for key areas of ministry in your church? Some of these key leaders will simply lead small groups. What if you spent a significant amount of time pouring into those leaders and making them great disciples and, by example, showing them how to disciple others? Those twelve could be shown how to disciple ten to twelve others serving in their ministries. Doing this increases the size of your church by ten.

At **Church Goals**, our goal is to equip you and provide training, mentoring, and coaching to help you become a thriving leader who can encourage and support your team, one who can encourage and support others. Disciples making disciples. We want to help you become an amazing pastor to hundreds or thousands on the weekend and an amazing pastor to your key leaders, who will pastor the multitudes in your church in turn. We want to help you reach the point where God will say, "Finally, I can trust you with the people I will send to your church."

Suppose you are a great self-starter and can take the ideas in this book and implement them in your church without any additional help or resources—GREAT! If you need a little extra help and would like a step-by-step plan and the specific resources to accomplish these ideas, please sign up for the **Church Goals** program. We promise it will help you, encourage you, and grow your church.

## YOU MIGHT WANT TO CONSIDER...

☐ Recruit ten to twelve key volunteers to lead ministries or small groups designed to meet felt needs.

☐ Pour into these ten to twelve leaders by discipling them and teaching them how to disciple others.

☐ If you need additional help...churchgoals.org.

## #2—HOW CAN YOU CONNECT PEOPLE TO YOUR SOLUTIONS FOR THEIR FELT NEEDS?

When people search the internet for a solution to their broken relationship or drug problem, they don't necessarily think Church might be their solution…until you put it right in front of them. Then the Holy Spirit goes to work and sparks an attraction to the idea that maybe the Church might provide some help. They will at least investigate the idea. That's why the churches in our **Church Goals** program are seeing 2,000–4,000 first-time visitors hit their website each month. Their church is one of the top options in a web search, and the searcher clicks through to the website to see what the church has to offer.

What if when people click through, it takes them right to a page that addresses their issue and their felt need (like the example I showed you in chapter 10 on Fixing Your Marriage)? You would have a fighting chance they might keep investigating and perhaps take the next step, like come to a DivorceCare class on Tuesday evening at your church because they just signed divorce papers. Or a **Business Goals** class on Thursday morning because they want to gain more leadership skills.

Getting people to your church will take a few steps. First, you must position your church on the first page and near the top when someone is searching for a solution on the internet. Then you must have a solution to their problem on your website. We discussed adding a landing page for each one of the felt needs for which your church is providing a solution. This is a page or area on your website dedicated to a specific topic. These are examples of categories or titles for landing pages:

**Landing Page Title Ideas Based on Felt Needs and Possible Objections**

| Marriage | Parenting | Finance | Loss/Grief | Addiction |
|---|---|---|---|---|
| Stress/Anxiety | Business/Work | Is God Real | Divorce | Fun |

To have an effective landing page, it must provide a logical next step. This could include making it very easy for them to visit a mid-week class or meeting on their topic of interest. It could also be a small group gathering. What is your church offering as solutions for peoples' felt needs? What will your landing pages connect them to?

## YOU MIGHT WANT TO CONSIDER...

- ☑ Figure out what your church will offer to meet the ten felt needs.
- ☑ Create landing pages on your website connecting them to the solution or area of interest they are searching for.
- ☑ Create an easy "next step" on your landing page, like inviting the viewer to a class, meeting, or small group in their area of interest.

## #3—HOW DO I ACTIVATE THE TROOPS GOD GAVE ME?

Have you considered that God has likely placed in your midst the people necessary to start the small group or lead the ministry that will be a solution for a felt need? Look for people in your church who have struggled through the ups and downs of marriage and figured out how to make it work. Those people could lead a small group of people wanting to work on their marriage. Are there people in your church who have struggled financially and are now passionate about helping others through what they went through? They could easily facilitate a financial class at your church. Are there others who have lost a loved one and can come beside someone else experiencing that? They could facilitate a grief class.

Here's the good news: there are great resources for everyone who wants to start a ministry or small group for each of the felt needs people are searching for. Nobody in your church needs to invent a curriculum and figure out how to lead a small group or start a ministry. Resources are abundant and already available. You just need to activate your troops.

Start with the Core Group meeting we discussed in chapter 9. Ask your Core Group whom God is calling your church to help. Then, ask each person at the meeting where they feel led to volunteer their time to help those people. This will help you develop a list of potential leaders and servants in your church willing to step up. You simply need to connect the dots—what are the needs, and who is willing to help? Pick two people to lead each small group or ministry and activate them.

You can start small. One couple will feel led to start the GriefShare ministry in your church. GriefShare is a vocational ministry that provides all the resources and training necessary for someone to start a ministry in your church for people experiencing grief. The couple can order the starter kit and undergo a very simple, self-paced training process. If they become available to just one person inside your church or someone from outside your church who is experiencing grief, that counts as success. GriefShare will list your church as a provider of its program, which could lead people to your church. You can also create a landing page on your church website that describes GriefShare in one or two paragraphs (GriefShare has the verbiage), which allows people to see your church as a potential solution for their grief when searching online. You can also add a link on connecting with the leaders of GriefShare and provide the day, time, and place of the next class.

Resources like GriefShare are available for all kinds of ministries and small groups you may want to start. You know you already have people inside your church who will step up and serve and won't need to invent anything themselves. You just have to ask them to get started. And if you need it, **Church Goals** can provide greater detail and step-by-step processes to activate, equip, encourage, and deploy the volunteers in your church. You just have to ask them and make it easy for them to sign up, get the tools and training they need, and make it easy for them to lead a small group or ministry. The nice thing about partnering with vocational ministries specializing in resources for small groups and ministries is that they have turn-keyed the process. They have developed all the training materials, curriculum, handouts, and marketing your church needs to successfully launch a small group or ministry with a volunteer and have it grow and become successful.

# YOU MIGHT WANT TO CONSIDER...

- ☑ Put leaders in place from the list of felt needs you created in the first section.
- ☑ Obtain the training materials and resources needed to equip your leaders.
- ☑ Think through your processes to make it easy for leaders to run their class, small group, or ministry. Consider room scheduling, how they'll access the building, or money transactions, and any needed equipment or copies.

# CAN YOU SUSTAIN GROWTH?

(SUSTAIN)

# 13

# WHAT WILL IT TAKE TO SUSTAIN GROWTH?

When your favorite sports team wins the national championship, are you anxious for the next season to start so you can see if they'll do it again? Don't you want them to sustain their success and have another championship season? God wants the same thing from you. When you have an amazing year—expanding the Kingdom with people coming to Christ—God wants you to do it again the next year.

You can change that even if you haven't experienced a "winning season" recently! If we look at the calendar year as the season, the year ends with Christmas—the "national championship." For our church, most decisions for Christ have always taken place at Christmas. For yours, it might be Easter.

Here's the best part, there is nothing more encouraging than leading people to Christ. If you have ten, twenty, or thirty more seasons in you, make it a goal right now to win ten, twenty, or thirty national championships—by making disciples each week and growing God's Kingdom.

## KEY QUESTIONS FOR THIS CHAPTER

1. Will you plateau?

2. How do you prevent plateauing?

3. What meetings should you hold to plan for the future—monthly, quarterly, and annually?

4. Do you have "A Year in Review"?

5. Do you create an Annual Calendar?

6. Do you hold a Ministry Fair Weekend?

7. Do you do a Small Group Weekend?

8. Is your Board focusing on the right things?

9. Do you inform your congregation and guests about giving...once a year?

10. Do you seek encouragement so you can encourage others?

## #1—WILL YOU PLATEAU?

Most churches plateau, even if it's just for a short time. What I mean by "plateau" is when we reach a stage where there is little to no change following periods of high activity or progress. The problem with plateauing is that we lose the momentum created from the high activity. It's like getting in peak physical condition to run a marathon, then you quit as soon as you finish the marathon. Once you are in shape, it's easy to keep running. The same is true with a church. Once you have growth momentum, it's much easier to keep growing and sustain that growth. But if you stop, it often takes so much time to rebuild the momentum again that everyone quits because it's too hard to ramp back up.

A component of the **Church Goals** program is to help churches set goals…and keep going. One goal might be to get to a certain size. If one church's attendance runs about seventy-five people on a Sunday, the church's goal might be to get to one hundred. So many times, we see the church reach that one hundred and then stop. Everyone breathes a sigh of relief and accomplishment, slowing down all the efforts they had deployed to reach their goal.

The problem is, I don't see in my Bible where it says, "Go and make disciples of all nations until you reach one hundred and then stop." Churches that grow do so because they are always focused on growing. If you reach your goal of one hundred, why not shoot for 150? When you reach 150, why not shoot for 300? When things are finally happening, people are coming, and their lives are being changed, keep it going. Why stop or slow down? The farmer's job is to grow. The fisherman's job is to fish. So keep growing, keep fishing!

The concept of momentum applies to small goals as much as big goals. Your big goal may be to reach one hundred people in church attendance, and a small goal supplements the larger goal, like holding a big event that brings people into your church. Let's say you decide to host the Car Show we discussed earlier. A lot of work goes into that type of event, and once it's over, you have a choice. You can kick back, put your feet up on the desk, and take a sigh of relief that it's over, or you have a celebration, take a short breather, and begin planning for the next event. Don't just have one fun service with a cool theme and then wait three months for the next one—make the next weekend fun, too. Yes, this takes work, but there's a payoff. You'll build momentum. People will come. Your church will grow.

You won't plateau.

We've talked to many churches who told us they ran that big event and had a great response…but they didn't run it again the next year. When we ask why they didn't run it again, we're told it took a lot of work. But just like going to the gym, it does take work for a while; then it becomes easier.

## YOU MIGHT WANT TO CONSIDER...

☑ Set a new goal the moment you reach your current goal.

☑ Celebrate the win you just achieved, take a short breather, then start working on the next year's event.

### #2—HOW DO YOU PREVENT PLATEAUING?

Asking yourself the five questions outlined in this book regularly and applying the solutions to each question can help you avoid plateauing and burnout. You can do this weekly regarding weekend services, monthly for your events, quarterly for your Core Group meetings, and yearly for annual planning and budgeting.

### THE FIVE QUESTIONS:

1. Am I still <u>called</u> to my position?
2. Am I <u>prepared</u> to grow?

3. Will I take the steps necessary to <u>grow</u>?
4. Will I <u>expand</u> in the areas necessary to grow?
5. Will I take the steps necessary to <u>sustain</u> the growth?

One way to do this is to simply start your week by saying, "I'm still called to run this church and to reach people for Christ, so what are we going to do to make this weekend amazing and introduce our new guests to Christ? How will we make it fun, relevant, and entertaining in a way that teaches God's Word deeply and meet the needs of everyone God sends through our doors?" Learn to embrace the call to grow your church and live up to God's call on your life. Live it out in your own life first, then with your team, and then with your congregation.

To sustain growth and prevent plateauing, you need to take care of yourself. How can you pour into the lives of others and encourage them if you aren't encouraged spiritually, physically, and emotionally? So many pastors are spiritually bankrupt because they expend all they have on others and don't put anything in their emotional bank accounts.

To avoid spiritual burnout, regularly take an internal check on your spiritual life. As David did in Psalm 139:23–24, ask the Lord to reveal anything in you that is wayward or offensive. Where are you spiritually downcast and negative? In which areas do you need to be strengthened? Consider your daily prayer life. Is it vibrant? Are you spending time each day with God, studying His Word, and listening for His guidance, direction, support, encouragement, cautions, and the love He has for you? Do you recognize the amazing things He's done in your life, the journey He's brought you on, and how He's masterfully put so many things in place for you to be successful and achieve His calling for you? Do you give Him thanks for those things?

Physical burnout needs to be addressed as well. Consider whatever physical activity energizes you and schedule that on your calendar daily. It often takes placing this activity on your calendar for twenty or thirty minutes to revive yourself physically and overcome the stress of the day.

Also, consider who supports you emotionally. Look around and notice whom God has placed to walk by your side. Who are the people that support and encourage you? Often the most obvious is our spouse. My wife has an amazing way of taking an emotional temperature of my day within a few minutes of me getting home. Then she knows exactly what to do to fill my tank emotionally. If I have a particularly hard day, she knows exactly what to say or do that calms me down and revive me. If your spouse isn't the person who can encourage you emotionally and fill your tank, identify who it is and ask if you can call them regularly for encouragement. Perhaps it's on your drive home. Maybe just a weekly call to that person can do it. When your emotional gas tank is full, you'll be better positioned to encourage and support others.

The foundation to sustaining growth and accomplishing everything God has called you to accomplish depends on taking care of yourself first. If you aren't doing that, stop everything and don't start again until you've implemented a self-care strategy. It will be life-changing. Please, do this today.

## YOU MIGHT WANT TO CONSIDER...

☑ Ask yourself these five questions on a regular basis:
- Am I still called to my position?
- Am I prepared to grow?
- Will I take the steps necessary to grow?

- Will I expand in the areas necessary to grow?
- Will I take the steps necessary to sustain the growth?

☑ Stay encouraged by having people in your life who support your positivity.

☑ Put in place a self-care plan that includes physical care, emotional care, and spiritual care

## #3—WHAT MEETINGS SHOULD WE HOLD TO PLAN FOR THE FUTURE—MONTHLY, QUARTERLY, OR ANNUALLY?

The processes outlined in this book follow God's design for growth, and we are called to do it yearly. We prepare the soil; we have a growing season; we reap a harvest; we rest, celebrate, and do it all over again. We've learned that if we prepare to grow each year, put some mechanisms in place that will continue to grow our church, take care of all the people that come, and prepare to do it again, we will continue to grow. You must do some things monthly, quarterly, or annually every year if you intend to grow. These include a Staff Retreat, Core Group Meetings, Leadership Core Meetings, and Vision Desserts.

### STAFF RETREAT

Start with an annual staff retreat where you can rest, have fun, spend time with God, and listen to His direction for the future. Invite anyone on your paid staff and all key volunteers and ministry or small group leaders. This should be the group of people whom you are discipling and pouring into.

This event will recharge your batteries and celebrate where God has brought you and what's been accomplished. Include the key people that will help you reach your goals. Start with a time of prayer and studying God's Word together. Then, break the day into three sessions—morning, afternoon, and after dinner. Devote one session to just having fun, one to discuss what went well and where you could use help, and one to dream about the future. Invite the Holy Spirit to preside over each session, so you accomplish what He wants you to accomplish—even with the session for having fun.

It's amazing what you can do in a day or two. Plus, these retreats don't have to be expensive. The key is to get away and not make this a meeting at "the office." Here's what the sessions could look like:

### Evaluate what went well and celebrate.

Ask everyone what they liked most about the past year. What was accomplished that should be celebrated? Where did your church impact the community and God's Kingdom? Have the group spend several minutes thinking about the past year and then write down responses on something everyone can see, like on a whiteboard or poster board. Star the items that everyone agrees should be repeated. At the end of this session, thank God for these achievements and His help in accomplishing them.

### Vision-casting

Ask everyone to spend a few minutes in prayer, asking God to reveal what people groups He wants your church to go after. What would God call you to accomplish in the next year or two if you knew that you couldn't fail? If there were successes you celebrated in the previous session, is God calling you to repeat those events or groups again to achieve a similar result? Go around the room, ask each person for one thing from their list, and add it to the whiteboard or poster board. Make a note of the ideas that are mentioned more than once. You'll begin to see how the Holy Spirit is moving. Continue around the room until every idea is on the board and how many times each idea is repeated. Circle the top four to five ideas and spend a few minutes in prayer over them.

## How will you accomplish these?

Start with prayer, asking God to reveal how to accomplish the four to five ideas that have been circled from the previous session. Have people spend about five minutes brainstorming ideas for how to accomplish each of them. Then, go around the room and have each person give one suggestion from their list. As with the previous session, keep track of suggestions multiple people mention. Once everything has been written and tabulated, circle the four to five suggestions that most people came up with. If some ideas involve funding that's not in the budget, that's okay. When you hold the Core Group meeting, you will address how to fund items the church doesn't have money for. Spend a few minutes in prayer over this session, thanking God for His direction and praying for the people and resources needed for the tasks.

## Staff and key volunteer commitments and assignments.

Next, ask people for prayer on who should lead and serve in each of the four to five areas identified in the previous session. Be praying about people in the room who should serve in an area and those in the church who are not at the retreat. Have God tell you, by name, whom He wants to serve in these areas. Write the four to five ideas from the previous session on a new whiteboard or poster board, then start making a list by going around the room and putting people's names next to the areas where people feel they should serve. Some might be obvious because you have a staff member or a key volunteer already overseeing a related area. That said, be open to having the Lord move people around. Don't let the person already in one area assume they will always be in that area. Be open to the guidance of the Holy Spirit.

## Have fun.

Plan this session so people can enjoy doing with they want to do. Don't assume everyone likes to hike. Make it free time with the caveat that people must have fun doing an activity of their choice together. You can easily do two work sessions in a day with a fun session in between. Consider doing a work session in the morning, a fun session all afternoon, and another work session in the evening. If you are doing a one-day retreat, you could do two sessions in the morning, have fun all afternoon, and do two sessions in the evening.

If you've been thinking about other things to accomplish in your church, like staff development, improvements, and other operational things, hold a second retreat or staff/volunteer meeting to address those things. They are important, and God will show you how to reach those things parallel to your church's mission. The purpose of the retreat is to celebrate and hear from God about the future direction of the church. This is the most important retreat. The next step is to affirm everything you think you've heard from God at your next Core Group meeting.

## YOU MAY WANT TO CONSIDER...

☐ Host an annual retreat with key staff, volunteers, and leaders to:
- Celebrate the prior year's accomplishments
- Determine what you should do next year
- Determine how to accomplish what should be done next year

## CORE GROUP MEETINGS

Remember that the Core Group is made up of leaders, key volunteers, potential leaders, long-time attendees, representatives from every age group, and anyone else who cares about the direction of your church. No one should feel excluded or that the Core Group is a private club closed to them. While we recommend holding Core Group and Leadership Core meetings (see below) four to six times a year, this particular meeting follows the annual retreat to confirm the church's direction.

With the Holy Spirit at work, those at your Core Group meeting should hear the same thing everyone who was at the retreat heard. It's imperative that you get everyone in your church on the same page relating to the mission, vision, and direction of your church. You can do that each year, starting with your Core Group meeting. We recommend holding the annual retreat described in the previous section sometime over the summer and this follow-up Core Group meeting at the end of summer or early September.

It's very important that you run the meeting from a blank slate like you never had your retreat. You don't want people thinking that everything has already been decided ahead of time. Instead, you are using the Core Group meeting as confirmation of what you think you heard from God at the retreat.

Run the meeting as described in chapter 8 and ask the same questions you asked at the retreat. List everyone's answers so everyone can see and follow the same process of working through the same five sessions (don't forget to build fun into your meeting). See if people who were not at the retreat come up with the same four to five ideas. Do they get the same support and following (i.e., do those ideas rise to the top as they did at the retreat)? Make sure people who were at the retreat don't lead with those ideas, but they can certainly affirm the ideas with their votes of confidence.

Having been at these meetings for over twenty years, it's amazing to watch the Holy Spirit work. The ideas are always aligned, and it's fun to see how God starts to hone those ideas into very specific directions with the right people stepping up to make them happen.

After the Core Group meeting, it's time to announce the four to five ideas to the congregation. On a Sunday morning, explain that through prayer and God's leading, the Core Group (which anyone is invited to) came up with four to five goals to focus on over the next year. Explain that it will take everyone in the church to achieve the goals God is asking you to accomplish.

If you would like a step-by-step instruction module on how to conduct the Core Group meeting, contact churchgoals.org for more information or to become part of the **Church Goals** program.

## YOU MAY WANT TO CONSIDER...

- ☑ Hold a Core Group meeting every year to get alignment with the 4–5 ideas from the annual staff retreat.
- ☑ Announce the 4–5 ideas that came from the Core Group meeting to your congregation and invite them to participate.

## LEADERSHIP CORE MEETINGS

In addition to the Core Group meeting in August or September, we recommend quarterly Leadership Core meetings. A Leadership Core meeting is a follow-up meeting to the Core Group meeting. These meetings are designed to keep your Core Leaders informed of the progress with the four to five initiatives identified and put into play from the Core Group meeting. It's also to get others in the church on board and serving and to thank everyone for their leadership and for serving. Thanking everyone for their service and for being a part of the church is very important.

These meetings follow the same outline we recommend for all staff/volunteer meetings, retreats, and Core Group meetings. After a time of prayer and thanksgiving, celebrate what God has done in your church since the previous meeting. This builds momentum. Then you report on what's going on right now. Give an update on the four to five initiatives relating to the progress that's been made, the people involved, and the events or weekly progress of the initiatives. Next, paint a vision for what's ahead, then finish by encouraging everyone to get on board either by serving or giving in support of one of the four to five initiatives.

We've seen that people start to look forward to the meetings because it shows the progress of the church and that they were part of a God-inspired movement. It shows the fruits of everyone's efforts. It also becomes a jumping-on point for anyone not already serving. We invite everyone in the congregation to become leaders in the church. Our goal is to get everyone serving in some capacity. We also want our volunteer leaders to recruit and invite people they know to come to the Leadership Core meeting.

Many times, we meet our annual goals earlier than predicted, and the Leadership Core meeting allows us to reset our goals, recruit more people for the project, and raise more money to reach the new goal(s).

The Leadership Core meetings should have a very festive atmosphere. They are celebrations, so they should be fast-paced and always have food, like spaghetti or pizza. At the church where I work, we hold them on a weeknight from 6:00 to 8:00 p.m. and always provide Children's Ministry (i.e., childcare) so families can come and not worry about babysitters. We even prepare run sheets for the event that keep things moving—down to the minute.

Holding the Leadership Core meeting at regular intervals allows you to make minor adjustments to your goals and allows you to recruit new people to become part of the Leadership Core. You want it to be something people feel honored to be part of and recognized for their leadership they've brought to your church. Also, invite people who have recently joined the church who have leadership skills and others who haven't been part of the Core yet.

Your Leadership Core should not be something that you screen for and hand-pick like you would for your Leadership Team (Elder Board). You want as many people as possible at your Leadership Core meetings. It would be okay if your whole church showed up, but don't just invite the whole church. Always announce it as a special meeting open to people who are leaders (or think they might be leaders), key volunteers (or think they might become key volunteers), and those who want to have a say in the future direction of the church.

## YOU MIGHT WANT TO CONSIDER...

- ☐ Hold Leadership Core meetings quarterly.
- ☐ Invite leaders, key volunteers, movers and shakers, and anyone with an opinion on the future direction of the church.

### VISION DESSERTS

What are your dreams for the future? Are people in your church aware of those dreams? Are there projects and initiatives in your church and community that you would like to accomplish in the next year? How do you fund new projects and initiatives? We recommend events we call Vision Desserts.

Each year, typically in November, we hold our annual Vision Desserts. We call them Vision Desserts because, well…we cast vision and serve dessert! At this point in the year, we've held our Core Group meeting in August or September to determine who God wants us to pursue. Next, we need to determine the initiatives, projects, and dreams we have for our church. We typically come up with five to ten projects, initiatives, and dreams, and formulate a plan and budget for each of them. Perhaps the Core Group meeting uncovered the need for a new paid staff member, like a youth pastor, who is not budgeted. You could bring this up at the Vision Dessert as a method to fund the youth pastor position if it wasn't funded at the Core Group meeting.

We invite small groups of people to come to a Vision Dessert where we unpack the five to ten ideas. Like the Core Group meeting, we start with prayer and ask the Holy Spirit to lead the evening. We then ask the group what initiatives and projects they like that the church has done in the past. Then we lay out the ideas we sense God is leading us to accomplish next. We ask everyone to pray for these initiatives, projects, hires, etc. and ask them to pray about supporting one or more financially. We lay out our financial goal and usually have support on some of the initiatives prior to the meeting (from our Board and key leaders that we may have spoken to prior to the Vision Dessert).

The Vision Dessert follows the same process a capital campaign would follow. We try to get a third to half of the money we need (seed money) before we go public with the event. This builds momentum for the initiative, and it shows people in the church that there are others who have stepped up to support it—giving it credence and support.

Vision Desserts ideally have between twenty to thirty people in attendance at each meeting. You want it to be a small enough group that people can engage in conversation about the projects and initiatives being discussed. If your church has one hundred people, try to fill two groups of thirty or three groups of twenty. We always count on a 35% no-show factor so allow for that in your plans.

After the Vision Dessert, we follow up with each person who attended to see if they have any follow-up comments and where they are feeling led to support either by prayer, financially, or both.

Vision Desserts should be an annual event. They unite the church, allow you to cast vision for the future, build momentum for the initiatives of the church, and remind people of the mission of the church.

## YOU MAY WANT TO CONSIDER...

☐ Hold Vision Desserts every year in November.
☐ Use your Vision Desserts to fund the initiatives developed at your Core Group meeting and other God-inspired plans for your church.

### #4—DO YOU HAVE A YEAR-IN-REVIEW?

People tend to forget the great things that are accomplished over the course of a year. If you put in place a solution for each of the questions in this book, you will have accomplished something significant. But most of the people in your congregation will forget them...unless you remind them. And reminding them will build a lot of momentum to do it again and to achieve what God is calling you and your church to accomplish.

Our recommendation is to plan a weekend service, either once or twice a year, that is a "Year-in-Review." These are fun, emotional, God-inspired, and God-glorifying weekends. A few weeks before this weekend, gather your staff, key volunteers, and leadership team (elders), and brainstorm all the great things that have happened in your church over the past year (or six months if you do this twice a year). As you are brainstorming, gather the statistics on the things you did, such as the cost, the number of people involved (how many came, how many served), who benefited or were touched, and the lives that were transformed. Collect any special stories about how lives were impacted. Even just one good story from each event or special day is fine.

Make a list of the following:

- ☑ Community service projects
- ☑ Special events (Vacation Bible School, Fall Halloween event, Christmas, Easter, holiday events, etc.)
- ☑ Special offerings (how much was raised, what was done with the money, and how it helped the recipients)
- ☑ New people coming to your church (special stories of those who have come to Christ and how it's transformed their lives, baptisms, baby dedications)
- ☑ Ministry successes (those you've started and how many people have benefited, such as Celebrate Recovery, GriefShare, DivorceCare, Strengthening Marriages, Business Goals, Youth Group, etc.)

At your Year-in-Review weekend, make sure to celebrate the great things God has done through everyone in your church. You want to thank God for what He's done in and through your church and thank the congregation for what has been accomplished. We usually build a slide show of photos to accompany the statistic. We also put a list of everything shown on the screen and put it in the bulletin along with a big "THANK YOU FOR MAKING THESE THINGS HAPPEN!" message.

Your sermon could include a few passages on God's provision or how God calls us to be compassionate to accompany your explanations of each statistic. You can tell a short story about each of the events. Your message should be divided into two parts: (1) events you were involved in, and (2) how lives were changed and/or how people started attending your church because of the events. While lives will be touched in both instances, the personal transformation of those who come to Christ can be very powerful and emotional.

For the events, your statistics and slides could look like this:

| EVENT | STATISTIC | PHOTO/SLIDE |
|---|---|---|
| Food Drive | 4,351 lbs. of food collected for food bank | Picture of food collected |
| School paint/repair | 16 people helped paint and bark (school) | People painting |
| Christmas Services | 267 in attendance, 12 accepted Christ | Photo of Christmas service |
| Easter | 329 in attendance, 17 accepted Christ | Photo of Easter service |
| Father's Day Car Show | 850 in attendance, 60 came to church | Photo of Car Show |
| Fire victims special offering | $4,000 raised | Photo giving a check to a cause |
| Vacation Bible School | 210 children attended/ 100 volunteers | Photo of kids having a blast |
| Adventure Sports | 23 regularly attending bike rides | Photo of mt. bike group |

| | | |
|---|---|---|
| Celebrate Recovery | 12 lives were changed | Photo of people praying (no faces) |
| Special Youth Event | 89 teenagers came to video game event | Photo of kids playing video |
| Marriage Retreat | 56 marriages were strengthened | Photo of event |

FATHER'S DAY CAR SHOW - 850 PEOPLE ATTENDED - 60 CAME TO CHURCH

List as many events and ministry highlights as you can think of, show a statistic for what happened at the event or ministry, and show a photo of the event or ministry. Be careful not to show the faces of people in sensitive ministries such as Celebrate Recovery.

For the part that's about lives being transformed, you can find and present stories in several different ways. You can ask each ministry to come up with the one to two most impactful or transformational stories from their ministry, then interview the person(s) from each ministry to tell their story and how their life was changed by the ministry.

The other thing we've done that has been super emotional and incredibly impactful is to collect around ten to twelve people whose lives were changed and put how their lives were changed on large cards (2'x2'). Show what their issue was before they came to church on one side of the card and the impact church had on the other side of the card. Each person walks out one at a time to the front of the stage, showing the front side of the card. After a brief showing of the front of the card, they turn it over to show how they've been transformed. It's very powerful and moving.

Here are some examples: A person walks out, and the front of the card says, "Got drunk almost every day." Then they turn the card over, and it says, "I've been sober for 97 days." Then they walk off the stage. The next person walks out, and the front of the card says, "Lost my husband." The back of the card says, "GriefShare gave me hope." Then they exit. The next person walks out, and the front of the card says, "Had no friends." The back of the card says, "I've found my new family at church."

The most powerful one I saw was when a man walked out, and the front of his card said, "Cheated on my wife and lost my family." The back of the card said, "Found Christ and got my family back." That was followed by his wife and kids, who only had writing on one side of the card. His wife's card said, "Got my husband back," and the three kids' signs each said, "Got my Daddy back." There wasn't a dry eye in the room. When you do the signs, have your worship team playing worship music quietly in the background—it can be recorded music if you don't have a worship team.

We've also incorporated a year-end review into our Christmas services to show the new visitors the kind of things our church does throughout the year. Since the New Year is just a week away, it provides a great finality to the previous calendar year.

The key to the Year-in-Review weekend is to remind people of how the Church changes and transforms the lives of people and to give thanks to everyone in your church for participating, for their generosity, and for making those life-changes possible.

People will be moved, grateful, thankful, and proud of their church, maybe even convicted for not giving or getting involved. But most importantly…they'll be glad to be connected to your church.

## YOU MIGHT WANT TO CONSIDER...

- ☑ Do an annual "Year in Review" in December as part of your Christmas services.
- ☑ Incorporate the most powerful visual…people walking out with the 2' x 2' cards described in this section.

### #5—DO YOU CREATE AN ANNUAL CALENDAR?

One of the keys to sustaining growth is to recognize the annual calendar and use it to your advantage to grow your church. There are days of the year the Church must own (Christmas and Easter), and there are other days we should stand out in our community. The culture you live in celebrates many special days in the year, so why shouldn't the Church? Your church is part of the community, after all, and can do something special on those days.

Christmas and Easter are Christian days of celebration and holidays in most countries. We should be prepared for the most visitors and the greatest opportunity to introduce them to the Church (and invite them back) because we have something of interest for them. If you need more information on how to "own" Christmas and Easter, we've put together a module called, "Christmas and Easter, Days We Should Own." Go to Churchgoals.org for more information.

In addition to Christmas and Easter, there are several other days of the year to bring awareness to the Church and invite people in. In the USA, we have Independence Day, Super Bowl Sunday, Valentine's Day, Mother's Day, Father's Day, St. Patrick's Day, Memorial Day, and Labor Day, just to name a few. Make them fun days with lots of activities and invite everyone in the community to join the celebration. For example, around the 4th of July, you could have hot dogs, hamburgers, and bounce houses for the kids. On Super Bowl Sunday, host a pancake breakfast and have everyone wear a jersey from their favorite football team. Honor anyone who has ever served in the armed forces on Memorial Day. Give flowers to all the women on Mother's Day and do a Car Show on Father's Day. These are just a few ideas.

In addition to the four seasons, recognize the New Year on the first weekend in January and the new school year in August or September. Both are great starting points for kicking off new initiatives that were hatched at the Core Group meeting. Have an official day in the spring when all children and youth groups move up to the next class. Use the seasons to your advantage.

Don't let momentum wane in the summer by using the excuse that everyone is on vacation. Yes, people take vacations, but the world doesn't stop. Our communities are still operating in the summer and so should the church.

In the summer, one of your greatest opportunities to reach people in your community is through a Vacation Bible School, which we call

Breakaway at our church. Our very first Breakaway had more people than we had in our church. We've learned that parents are looking for places to drop their kids off in the summer, and the church is a perfect spot. It's safe and trusted, and their children might hear something good. Vacation Bible School can be a few hours in the morning or a few hours in the afternoon or all day long. There are a lot of resources on the web for how to put on a Vacation Bible School, and the **Church Goals** program has a module on that too.

You can use the seasons God created to stop one thing and launch another. You can use the special days in each season as a time to do something special in the church and invite everyone in your community. What will your annual calendar look like?

## YOU MIGHT WANT TO CONSIDER...

☑ Create an annual calendar and highlight the "days you will own."

☑ Consider what special days or events you can create around the seasons.

## #6—DO YOU HOLD A MINISTRY FAIR?

How do you recruit volunteers? So many pastors tell us they can never get enough people to serve as volunteers in the church. Our answer: the Ministry Fair.

The Ministry Fair is a series of tables representing every ministry in the church. Each year we select a weekend to do the Ministry Fair with the sole purpose of getting at least half of our church to sign up to serve in some capacity. We preach about Christ's servant heart and our desire to be more like Christ. We keep the sermon short, no more than twenty minutes, and we end with a charge for everyone to sign up somewhere to serve in the church. We then direct them outside to our Ministry Fair.

When the congregation is released, they are encouraged to visit every ministry table to find the one that piques their interest. Each ministry is encouraged to decorate its table in a way that highlights the ministry. Have existing volunteers dress up in matching t-shirts and help at the table to recruit new volunteers.

It's a very festive event. We have music playing in the background, some kind of food available, like hot dogs and hamburgers, and some fun activities for the kids, like bounce houses, face painting, or carnival games.

Volunteerism in the church is critical, and you need to be deliberate about how you recruit them. You won't be able to sustain the events and initiatives your church is involved in without a strong volunteer base. The Ministry Fair is just one way to develop this.

## YOU MIGHT WANT TO CONSIDER...

☐ Hold a Ministry Fair twice a year to recruit volunteers.

## #7—DO YOU HOLD A SMALL GROUP WEEKEND?

You have a very good shot at making visitors lifelong members if you can get them to do three things:

1. Come to church on Sunday
2. Serve as a volunteer
3. Join a Small Group

Small Groups (also called Life Groups or Discipleship Groups in some churches) must become a cornerstone in your church. When people get into small groups, they find their community and support mechanism. As you might have guessed, an important module in the **Church Goals** program is our Small Groups Module. We provide detailed information on how to start, maintain, or expand the Small Groups ministry at your church.

It's such an important part of our sustained growth plan that we hold Small Groups Weekends twice a year. The design and run sheet for the weekend is nearly identical to the Ministry Fair. We hold a short (twenty-minute) service, preach on the importance of small groups, and dismiss everyone to go outside where we have tables with small group leaders. The congregation is encouraged to go from table to table until they find a group they want to visit. We also have tables for those wanting to join with others to start new groups.

Tables are labeled according to the type of group, which could be life stage (e.g., young professionals, newly married, parents with young children, empty nesters), location (where the group meets), day and time the group meets, any special interest (think Adventure Sports), etc. We also put together a list of groups that we print out with all of the above information so people can find the group they might be interested in and talk with them. Our website also has a mechanism for people to find and sign up for groups.

## YOU MIGHT WANT TO CONSIDER...

- ☑ Find two great volunteers to lead your Small Groups ministry.
- ☐ Hold a Small Group Weekend twice a year.
- ☐ Aim to get 80% of the people in your church into a small group

### #8—IS YOUR BOARD FOCUSING ON THE RIGHT THINGS?

John Carver is considered by many to be the leading authority on nonprofit and corporate boards. Carver makes a point that most boards are underutilized and focused on the wrong things. It's up to you to get them focused on what's most important.

Your board will discuss whatever you put on the agenda. For many churches, their agenda is duplicated from the month before with only the dates changed. This can go on for years with only minor adjustments to the agenda. Yet the purpose of the board is to wrestle with how your church is going to fulfill its mission to go out and make disciples. Often too much time is spent discussing trivial things like whether the $10 reimbursement for coffee with a congregant was the best use of the pastor's time and church funds.

An effective church board might prioritize and weigh their role, responsibility, and authority as follows:

☑ Confirm mission and vision (90%)

☑ Long-range dreaming (8%)

☑ Control heresy (1%)

☑ Church discipline (1%)

By extension, the board should focus an appropriate amount of time on each of those four priorities.

To sustain growth, you need to have a board that supports growth and is passionate about going out and making disciples—your primary mission. Your board will likely support growth once you hold the Core Group meeting.

## YOU MIGHT WANT TO CONSIDER...

☑ Read *Boards That Make A Difference: A New Design for Leadership in Nonprofit and Public Organizations*, Jossey-Bass, 2006.

☑ Make the most of what you have on your board agenda consent items so you can spend most of the time figuring out how to reach the goals established at your Core Group meeting and annual retreat — your mission.

## #9—DO YOU INFORM YOUR CONGREGATION AND GUESTS ABOUT GIVING...ONCE A YEAR?

We know one of the complaints the unchurched have about coming to church is they will be asked for money. We also know that not everyone in your church has the right perspective on giving. Why not overcome both of those problems and explain the biblical perspective on money?

When you let your visitors off the hook when it comes to giving (see chapter 8), you will temporarily eliminate that obstacle they use for not wanting to come to church. But the issue needs to be revisited at some point. We recommend dedicating one weekend sermon each year to the biblical perspective on giving. There are two benefits to this weekend's topic. First, you will remind your congregation about their responsibility to tithe, and you will inform your new members or visitors what it means to give.

Money is one of those things that often isn't talked about in church yet is a big deal to God and a big deal to people. I call money the root of one of the three "big rock" sins in the Bible—greed. The other two "big rock" sins are power/pride and sex. But money can also become a source of many blessings. When people hear God's perspective on money, how to manage and handle it, and the blessing that comes with giving instead of receiving, it changes their perspective on tithing.

We've used Robert Morris's book *The Blessed Life* (Gospel Light, 2009) as a resource for our sermons on giving and have had amazing responses from our congregations. For the past twenty-five years, our senior pastor has challenged people to start tithing with a money-back guarantee...if their life doesn't improve, the church will refund 100% of the money they tithed, no questions asked. In twenty-five years, only three people requested their money back.

We like to do the sermon on giving in the first few weeks of January. It's a new year, we get several people coming back after visiting the church for the first time at Christmas, and January is traditionally a low month for giving. (I think a lot of people feel they gave big at the end of the calendar year and can take a little break from giving in January.)

## YOU MIGHT WANT TO CONSIDER...

- ☑ Dedicate one weekend message a year to giving.
- ☑ Give people a guarantee that their life will improve when they become obedient to tithing...offer their money back anytime during the first year if they don't see a positive change in their lives.

### #10—DO YOU SEEK ENCOURAGEMENT SO YOU CAN ENCOURAGE OTHERS?

Your church will not grow if you are not encouraged and, in turn, encourage others. It's one of your primary roles as a pastor or ministry leader. Yet so many pastors we meet are discouraged, and what's worse, they don't know how to encourage others.

When you were growing up, were your father and mother encouraging to you? Many pastors and leaders did not have a good example of an encouraging parent growing up and now don't know how to encourage others. But you need to learn how you get encouraged, and you need to encourage others. According to Oxford, the definition of encouragement is the action of giving someone support, confidence, or hope.[3] Encouragement is an action that can be learned. It takes a little practice and may feel foreign or awkward at first, but being an encourager can become natural and genuine.

If we just take the definition, it tells us how we can be encouraging (by doing one or more of the following):

☑ Give the person support

☑ Give the person confidence

☑ Give the person hope

You are probably encouraging when you preach, as most messages contain one or more of these three elements. Here are some tips for becoming encouraging in one-on-one conversations.

***You can give people support by:***

☑ Affirming their skills and talents, verbalizing what they are good at

☑ Listening intently when they want to tell you something

☑ Telling them you care about them and they are valuable

☑ Inspiring them in the areas they excel

☑ Spending time with them

---

[3] "encourage," Google.com. https://www.google.com/search?q=definition+of+encourage&oq=definition+of+encourage&aqs=chrome..69i57j0i67j0i20i263i512j0i512j0i22i30j69i60j69i61l2.4426j1j4&sourceid=chrome&ie=UTF-8.

*You can give people confidence by:*

☑ Reminding them of their past successes

☑ Helping them overcome their doubts

☑ Telling them you trust them

☑ Recognizing them when they succeed

☑ Believing in them and their abilities

*You can give them hope by:*

☑ Putting their trust in God

☑ Making them aware of God's faithfulness

☑ Reminding them that God keeps His promises to us

☑ Taking an inventory of the positives in their life

☑ Praying for them

What if you put a rule in place in your life that said you had to deploy something from the above list in every interaction you had with another person from now on? What if you tried to do one from each category? What if you prayed to God before or during every interaction with someone that He would give you the words of encouragement to give the other person? What if you committed to not finishing a conversation with anyone without incorporating something encouraging for them? If you did each of those things, you will be an encouragement to everyone you meet.

If you were not encouraged growing up and therefore think you can't be an encouragement to others, use that to your advantage. Think about how you wanted to be encouraged and practice giving that encouragement to others. God will put people in front of you that you are uniquely equipped to encourage.

Finally, determine how you like to be encouraged and what is encouraging to you, and make sure you get some dose of that every day. This will give you what you need to sustain your ministry and God's call on your life.

## YOU MIGHT WANT TO CONSIDER...

☑ Set a rule that you will be encouraging in every conversation you have.

☐ Have a conversation with every person who reports to you that is designed to encourage them. Once a week is best, and once a month is the least effective. Anything outside of monthly will result in you being labeled as someone who is not encouraging.

# PUTTING IT ALL TOGETHER

# THE SUM OF ALL THE PIECES

Are you beginning to see that a lot goes into making your church grow? The solution won't be in any single component discussed in this book but the sum of all the pieces. Look at everything God has placed in your hands to advance His Kingdom. You have everything you need to be successful! God wants you to start a process that will get you and everyone in your church to go after the lost in your community—*to go out and make disciples.*

---

**KEY QUESTIONS FOR THIS CHAPTER**

1. What does God want you to start?
2. When does God want you to stop?

---

## #1—WHAT DOES GOD WANT YOU TO START?

I've given you multiple steps you can take to grow your church, and you may be overwhelmed at this point with so many things to do. We recommend planning for changes in your church in very small and manageable steps over the next year, one step per quarter. If you want the most simplistic breakdown of the summary of this book, what the **Church Goals** program does most successfully, it's this:

*Step One:* **PREPARE** *your church*

☑ Prepare every aspect of your church for first-time visitors, including your website, campus, volunteers, sermons, and social media.

☑ Compel everyone in your church to go after those in your community who do not know Christ.

The first quarter process to PREPARE your church for growth can be simplified to just this: Run a Core Group meeting and ask and answer ONLY the four questions outlined in chapter 8.

*Step Two:* **GROW** *your church*

☑ Connect the thousands of people searching the internet daily for solutions to their desires or problems to your church.

☑ Pick just two or three areas people are searching for solutions and deploy those solutions in your church.

The second quarter process to GROW your church can be summarized by this: Use the internet, specifically Google, to show the world that your church has what they are looking for—a solution to their felt need. Pick just two or three of the ten felt needs that people are looking to solve in their lives and highlight them on your website, social media, and in your community.

*Step Three: **EXPAND** your church*

- ☑ Put in place ministries or small groups as the solutions to the two or three felt needs people in your community are looking for.
- ☑ Utilize the gifted people God has already placed in your church to help you lead these ministries or small groups…as volunteers.

The third quarter process to EXPAND your church can be summarized by this: Activate and deploy the people God has already placed in your church who are gifted in certain areas to volunteer and run the two or three ministries or small groups in your church that meet the felt needs of the people in your community.

*Step Four: **SUSTAIN** your church's growth.*

- ☐ Ask God to inspire new growth goals every year.
- ☐ Re-deploy the successful sermons, events, gatherings, and meetings that brought great results in the previous year.

The fourth quarter process to SUSTAIN growth in your church can be summarized by this: You will see growth, and people will come to your church and stay as a result of your first three quarters presented (PREPARE, GROW, EXPAND). You will experience the same levels of growth and success if you do much of what you did in the previous nine months in the following year.

## #2—WHEN DOES GOD WANT YOU TO STOP?

God won't want you to stop until everyone in your community hears the word of God and is given a chance to make a decision for Christ. That may take all your lifetime and a few more. The charge to go out and make disciples was given by Christ over 2,000 years ago, and faithful ministers of the Gospel have been doing their best to do that ever since. God has blessed those who do their best to live up to their calling, and the same will happen with you. You will win games every weekend, and you will win national championships every year. By the way, who are you playing against every weekend and in every national championship? Satan. Not other churches and not other pastors. Satan's team is the world, and they don't want you to win. But we have a supernatural star player on our team who can win every game. His name is Jesus, and He can influence every single player on your team and make each one of them, and you, mini-super heroes. You just have to activate Jesus, through the Holy Spirit, in each one of your players, then deploy them into the game. Commit today to start winning games and national championships. You can do it!

I doubt you read any of the questions in this book and the solutions in the "You might want to consider…" sections and said, "There's no way that will work." On the contrary, the Holy Spirit has already been encouraging you that if you do what is suggested, your church will grow. People will start coming to your church and allow you to lead them to Christ. You will become more encouraged every day. Take it one day at a time, spend about an hour each week, and watch what happens.

I would welcome you to connect with me to share how these ideas have helped you personally and with your church and ministry. I look forward to hearing about your success!

# THE BOOK IN THIRTY MINUTES

This is a summary of the key questions asked in this book. Read each question, and ask God what the right answer is for you.

### Introduction

1. Does God want you to accomplish something significant in your lifetime?
2. Do you think God has equipped you to accomplish something significant?
3. Might you accomplish this through your church or where He has placed you?
4. Do you think God will use your past experiences, expertise, and giftings to accomplish whatever He wants you to accomplish?
5. Do you think we are called to reach the lost and make disciples?
6. Have you been doing all the right things to accomplish what God would like you to accomplish? Might you need to make a few adjustments?

### The Five Key Questions

1. Are you called? (AFFIRM)

2. Are you prepared? (PREPARE)

3. Do you know how to grow? (GROW)

4. Are you willing to expand? (EXPAND)

5. Can you sustain growth? (SUSTAIN)

### Chapter One—Affirm Your Calling

1. Did God call you into (this) ministry?

2. Is there someplace you'd rather be?

3. Do you know what you were called to accomplish?

### Chapter Two—Do You Know Who Your Flock Is?

1. Has God charged you to shepherd only those in your church?

2. Whom has God placed in your midst to help you?

3. Is your ministry just about moving peas on the plate?

4. Is your church primarily a hospital for the hurting or a home for the healthy?

### Chapter Three—Are You Called to Go and Make Disciples?

1. Do I actually have to go after the lost?

2. Who will do the discipling?

3. Am I supposed to make disciples by myself?

### Chapter Four—Why Aren't People Coming to Your Church?

1. Is your church ready for God to send new visitors?

2. What experience do you have with being unchurched?

3. Have you ever been a first-time visitor?

4. Why don't people come to church?

5. Does your church have what they are looking for?

6. Do you and the people in your church want your church to grow?

## Chapter Five—Where Is Your Focus?

1. Have you become too comfortable?

2. Have you become distracted from your mission?

3. Are you focusing on what's most important?

## Chapter Six—Are You Ready for Visitors?

1. Is your church ready for visitors?

2. Is your website ready for visitors?

3. Is your church visitor-friendly?

4. Who are you speaking to? (First-timers, relatively new people, the congregation, leaders)

5. Are you teaching in all four learning styles?

6. What do the social media channels say about your church?

7. How are the reviews on your church?

## Chapter Seven—Is Your Church Relevant?

1. What do people want and need?

2. Are you preaching on relevant issues?

3. Are you addressing felt needs in the sermon?

4. Where do timing and relevance converge?

## Chapter Eight—What Will It Take to Prepare for Visitors?

1. How will you get everyone on board, including yourself?

2. Will a visitor understand what's going on?

3. Will you need to become a better preacher?

4. Will you need to become a better leader?

### Chapter Nine—Do People Know You Exist?

1. Do people know you exist?

2. Are you open to "everyone else?"

3. Do you have an inviting culture?

4. Are you active in your community?

5. How is your online presence?

### Chapter Ten—What Will It Take to Grow?

1. Where does growth come from?

2. Is your church findable?

3. Where are people looking?

4. What are they looking for?

5. How can your website help you grow?

6. Have you thought about the business community?

7. How can social media help you grow?

8. Are vocational ministries welcome at your church?

### Chapter Eleven—Do You Have What People Are Looking For?

1. What are you doing for people looking for a social outlet and community?

2. What are you doing for people looking for a mission or purpose?

3. Are you giving people an excuse to come to church?

4. How can you make your church fun with interesting services?

**Chapter Twelve—Will You Expand in the Areas Necessary to Grow?**

1. Does your church have ministry solutions for some or all of the ten felt needs?
2. How can you connect people to your solutions for their felt needs?
3. How do I activate the troops God gave me?

**Chapter Thirteen—What Will It Take to Sustain Growth?**

1. Will you plateau?
2. How do you prevent plateauing?
3. What meetings should you hold to plan for the future—monthly, quarterly, and annually?
4. Do you have a "Year-in-Review"?
5. Do you create an Annual Calendar?
6. Do you hold a Ministry Fair Weekend?
7. Do you do a Small Group Weekend?
8. Is your Board focusing on the right things?
9. Do you inform your congregation and guests about giving... once a year?
10. Do you seek encouragement so you can encourage others?

**Chapter Fourteen—The Sum of All the Pieces**

1. What does God want you to start?
2. When does God want you to stop?

# ABOUT JUD BOIES AND CHURCH GOALS

Jud Boies is the Executive Director and Pastor of the **Church Goals** and **Business Goals** ministries. Jud has built a team dedicated to helping churches reach the multitudes of people in their community who don't know Christ. Jud served nine years as the Executive Pastor of Operations at Bayside Church in Northern California (which was ranked the #1 fastest-growing church in America by Outreach Magazine in 2019 during his tenure) and has been consulting with churches using the **Church Goals** program since 2005. The **Church Goals** program works with churches from any denomination and is committed to keeping every aspect of the church's DNA, liturgy, culture, and history intact—not changing 1% of it.

Jud has over thirty years of business experience at the C-Level. He is passionate about helping re-energize churches and showing people how to integrate their faith into leadership roles in the church and the workplace. He graduated from the University of California, Berkeley, and has a master's degree from Western Seminary. Jud has been married to his wife, Mary, since 1982, and together they have twin daughters and a granddaughter.

# BUSINESS
# GOALS

If you want to launch the **Business Goals** ministry at your church or want more information, go to businessgoals.org for more information. You may also scan this QR code:

*Goals* is a resource for anyone in the workplace who wants true success at work and home. Designed after the **Business Goals** program, Jud Boies developed this practical guide for achieving what we want most while building relationships along the way. This book follows the life of Todd Hanson, a fictional character who reaches amazing success through the **Business Goals** program. Everything Todd goes through has happened in real life to people who have adopted the principles in this unique system.

For over twenty-five years, the **Business Goals** program has been deployed in the lives of thousands of people in companies such as

Intel, Apple, Google, Chick-fil-A, and FedEx. In every case, the results are measurable. Most people reach significantly higher levels of success because they achieve their goals and objectives while strengthening the most important thing in their life—their relationships. You can, too.

In *Goals*, you will learn how to:

- enjoy the people you work with;
- get the most out of your marriage;
- achieve your goals for income and advancement;
- become the dream parent to your kids;
- get what you want most at work and at home.

To order your copy, visit Amazon.com or wherever books are sold.